Are you Crying?

ABOUT THE AUTHORS

Rev. Seotaek Joo has significantly impacted Korean churches in particular, and the rest of society in general, with his vision for student ministry, social welfare, and the inner healing ministry. He was with the Campus Crusade for Christ Korea (Cru Kor) for 25 years, serving in various capacities as the Executive Vice President, President of Mission in Korea, and Co-President of the Campus Gospel Organization, among others.

For his impact on society, Rev. Joo was awarded the Order of Civil Merit by President Dae Jung Kim, the eighth president of Korea. The Government of Korea also selected him as one of 157 persons who brought hope to Koreans, and one of 50 who impacted Chung-Cheong state. Furthermore, Rev. Joo was awarded the Grand Citizen Prize by the Chung-Cheong state government and the Grand Culture Prize by the Cheong-Ju city government. Rev. Joo likewise received an Honorary Doctoral Degree in Theology from the New York Theological Seminary.

In 2002, Rev. Joo left Cru Kor and founded the Lord's Church in downtown Cheong Ju, a neighborhood known for its strip clubs and bars. The revival of the Lord's Church, which he initiated, had a crucial impact on its neighborhood. Since then, the Lord's Church has practiced a reformative model of a church that grows and shares with others outside the church and the rest of the neighborhood. After several years, Rev. Joo retired early from his post as senior pastor. He currently serves as Pastor Emeritus.

Dr. Sunwha Kim majored in nursing and social welfare and conducted further studies at London Bible College and ACTS University. Furthermore, she received her doctoral degree in healing missiology, an interdisciplinary study on theology, psychology, and medical science, at Konyang University, making her the first healing missiologist in Korea. She previously served as the Executive of Counseling at Cru Kor. At present, she focuses on conducting research and providing lectures and training for a Christian counseling program. She is the concurrent president of the Biblical Inner Healing Ministry Center.

Rev. Joo and Dr. Kim initiated their inner healing ministry vision in 1992 with the first Biblical Inner Healing Seminar in Korea. The seminar has been held regularly since then, attracting around 60,000 people, including those who attended the 152nd Biblical Inner Healing seminar held in June 2022.

Together, Rev. Joo and Dr. Kim have designed training materials for the seminar and published several books, including *Mom, Please Don't Leave Me, Asking in Confusion, Memory Attack, Wounds and Hurts that Need to be Healed Before Marriage, Only in Faith,* and *Inner Healing with Paintings and the Bible.*

Translated from the Korean
by Bora Joo

Are you Crying?

Biblical Theory and Cases of
Inner Healing

SEOTAEK JOO

SUNWHA KIM

SOOP TO NAMU

Are you crying?

내 마음 속에 울고있는 내가 있어요

by Seotaek Joo and Sunwha Kim

Originally published in 1997 in the Republic of Korea

Copyright © 1997, 2015 by Seotaek Joo and Sunwha Kim

English Translation Copyright © 2022 by Bora Joo

Translated from the updated edition published in Korean in 2015.
First published on December 1, 2022 in the Republic of Korea

All rights reserved. No part of this publication may be reproduced or transmitted in any form or by any means without prior permission in writing from the publishers

SOOP TO NAMU

137 Naesudong-ro, Cheong-Ju, Chungbuk, Republic of Korea

ISBN 979-11-978422-2-1 (03230)

Book design by Bora Joo

Our beloved daughter Dr. Bora Joo experienced a deeper dimension of God's presence while she was translating this book. This is our greatest joy.

CONTENTS

Preface to the English edition: The journey of finding myself in Jesus Christ	15
Me, crying inside myself	19
A theoretical basis for Biblical Inner Healing and counseling: The New Covenant Model	31

Session 1 What is Biblical Inner Healing? 41

    Case God found and came to me, hiding in a barley field 59

    Case Please let me die or allow me to divorce him 63

    Case God wiped off the food waste on my body 67

Session 2 Knowledge vs. Relationship 71

Session 3	**Who am I?**	83
Case	Knowing who I am in God gave me freedom	98
Session 4	**What does the Bible say about human beings?**	103
Session 5	**Bitter root and forgiveness**	127
Case	What? I am not your mom	140
Case	How I was healed from my persistent stomach pain	143
Case	Arrows in my heart and God's heart	145
Session 6	**Be filled with the Holy Spirit**	147
Case	I was about to give up being a Christian	158
Case	What changed me was not the thirty years of education but three days of Bible study	162
Session 7	**The bonds that keep you away from your true father**	165
Case	God hung out with me at the empty playground	185
Case	My food allergy has disappeared	189

Session 8	**The spiritual warfare inside me**	193
Case	You ended your mother's life	211
Case	You have a dual personality	215
Case	How the curse of Satan shaped my life	217
Session 9	**Jesus came into the world to meet you**	221
Case	I also suffered from poverty, just like your father	237
Case	They also called me demon-possessed.	240
Case	The story of a teacher	244
Session 10	**From healing to growth**	247
Case	It is too heavy to carry	266
Case	A knife in my hand	272

Sexual issues that cause severe damage and the Inner healing		283
Case	Story of A, B, and C	285

PREFACE TO THE ENGLISH EDITION

The journey of finding myself in Jesus Christ

There is sorrow, loneliness, and sadness inside each of us. So, we tend to search for an all-encompassing warmth that can hold us.

"Is God real?"

"Is God interested in me?"

Many Christians feel nervous, anxious, and sorrowful like orphans while they call God "Father God." Do these feelings mean that God is incompetent? Do they indicate that God does not care how we feel?

Biblical inner healing is to know and experience God as practical help and a healer for our wounded hearts. This is one of God's essential promises in the Gospel of the Cross.

We developed the New Covenant Model, a psychological model based on the binding promises of Jesus Christ. Based on the model, we have regularly held the Biblical Inner Healing seminar for the past thirty years. So far, more than 60,000 people have attended the seminar. We have visited hundreds of churches here and abroad for the inner healing ministry.

Missionaries shared the contents of this book with indigenous peoples in the Amazon jungle and witnessed the amazing work of the Holy Spirit in them. Readers of this book from around the world, including Japan, Norway, and Sweden, shared their testimonies, praising the incredible work of the Holy Spirit in their lives.

The Bible states that every man's heart is broken, imprisoned, and locked up. Only the Gospel of Jesus Christ and the actual help of the Holy Spirit can heal their broken heart.

This book contains vivid stories of people who have experienced God as a healer for their personal and psychological issues. We have witnessed how the healing changed their personality and lives. When people experience God as a healer for their broken hearts, it changes them to truly believe that they are from God and God is with them.

We initiated this vision of biblical inner healing in 1992 and have held the Biblical Inner Healing seminar every year since then, with continued passion and grace from God.

Our daughter, Bora, has accompanied us in this journey and greatly helped us with this book as an English translator. Youngkwang, Minsu, and Won have supported and prayed for us. Most of all, God has been with us.

We pray for all readers of this book to experience the work of the Holy Spirit and meet God as a healer of their wounded hearts, as it was promised in the Gospel of the Cross.

Seotaek Joo and Sunwha Kim
October, 2022

Me, crying inside myself

It was five in the morning, and Yoone woke up to a dark and cold day. She left her friend and decided to walk down the street. After taking several steps, she felt something even colder than the weather. It was something inside her—a sense of great loneliness tinged with deep sorrow.

"Where are you now?" Yoone's mom asked her on the phone.

"I am at a bar," She answered. Yoone lied exactly because she knew it would upset her mom. Having said that, she was swept by some kind of mixed feelings. Soon, Yoone was overwhelmed by guilt and sadness. It was not the first time she had lied to her mom, saying she was at the bar. Yoone couldn't explain why she wanted to make her mom feel miserable, even with lies.

She continued walking, thinking to herself, 'Maybe I am full of evil. Grandma said I am the saboteur of my family.' Guilt just filled her mind. 'Maybe Grandma was telling the truth. Yes, I am the child who makes my parents miserable. I'm not a child who brings joy.'

When Yoone got home, her mom was waiting for her without the lights on. She was sitting quietly in the dark.

"Where are you coming from?"

"...."

"We need to talk."

"About what?" Yoone answered angrily.

"Mom, I am moving out. I don't want to live here any longer!"

Yoone knew that her words were becoming harsh. The guilt that she felt throughout the night was no longer there. She thought to herself, 'How dare she want to talk with me? Now, she wants to be a good mom after all those times?'

Yoone couldn't understand why she felt this intense hostility toward her mom. In fact, whenever she heard her mom's soft voice, it just seemed to make her more furious, to the point that she could no longer control what came out of her mouth. At that moment, she couldn't even control her body, and she soon passed out.

She only remembered the stunned look on her mom's

face when she woke up.

When Yoone opened her eyes, she immediately felt miserable. The sad and concerned look of her family surrounding her made her feel like a monster. The guilt came back, overwhelming her.

'Why do I even say those words to my mom? Do I have a mental illness? Is there some monster inside me? Oh God, please help me,' Yoone desperately asked.

Yoone and her family couldn't understand how such intense rage surged through her. Her family invited an exorcist and even brought her to a shrink. Over the days, Yoone's fury became more intense, and her mind and body became increasingly weaker until both her legs were paralyzed. Finally, her family brought her to a church, and it was the pastor who told them that Yoone was possessed by a demon. Immediately, they arranged for Yoone to join the special prayer program for three days. However, she didn't get better.

It was a cold winter when I first met Yoone, who came with her sister. Yoone's sister, who studied Chi energy for years, said, "We need to try something different. Please help my sister."

Yoone, who sat on a couch in my living room, said:

"I see myself crying inside my heart. Here, at the left side of my heart. I see a little girl crying inside me, and it's me. I don't see her legs, but she has long black hair and a pale face. She's crying. I know it's me, but I don't know why she's crying. I see her crying inside me, even when

I am smiling outside. I see the grief on her face. She's always crying. I feel like she's going to die because she cries too much. I don't know what to do."

Is Yoone possessed by some demon or ghost, as her family thinks? Or does she go through a nervous breakdown due to her weak Chi energy, as her sister thinks?

A week after, Yoone joined the Biblical Inner Healing Seminar (BIH Seminar). On the second day of the seminar, there was a small group session sharing thoughts from the sessions. One lady shared her story, and it triggered Yoone to think about her issue from a new perspective.

The lady told her story about her relationship with her daughter.

My daughter is in kindergarten, so it is not easy to raise her like any other kids. But she says some words that scare me. She sometimes tells me that she wants to make me feel miserable. I was shocked when I first heard this because it is not something a little kid usually says to her mom. So I asked someone known for spiritual gifts to pray for my daughter. And I was told that my daughter is possessed by a demon. I didn't believe it when I was told. But I see that it affected how I see her and my love for her. I started to dislike my daughter, and she got worse. I know that I should not dislike my child. Something terrible will happen if I continue not to like my baby. I don't know what I should do. So I came to the BIH seminar.

Today, during the session, I realized for the first time

that it was me who was having an issue and not my child. God showed me the cause of the issue in a way that no one else could.

I saw a scene in my mind during the session. There was a young girl, and it was myself when I was young. I was standing alone, and there was a huge piece of wood that was getting close to me. I wanted to run away, but I had no place to go. Soon, I realized it was actually my mom who was holding this "log." The vision became more explicit. It was a memory that happened when I was young. I don't remember why, but I think I didn't listen to my mom in front of other people. My mom thought I was being disrespectful and decided to spank me. At first, she used a thin ruler, but when the ruler broke, she came with that piece of wood. While she was spanking me, I knew it was not because I did something wrong. This was because her pride was damaged in front of other people. Strangely, I felt like that "log" spanked me by itself, not by my mom.

At first, I didn't understand why I recalled this memory, but during the prayer session, God told me why. I thought God had shown this to me at a time when my relationship with my mom was completely over. I have never felt love from my mom. Likewise, I didn't give love to my child, and my daughter was angry because of this. As she got mad, I hated her more, thinking she was possessed by a demon. Later on, I realized that this was a vicious cycle.

Now, I know I was wrong, and this knowledge broke

my heart. Before my daughter was born, I swore to be a good, loving mother—unlike my mom. Ironically, I can see now that I am even worse than my mom.

It was the time when Yoone started crying, wailing like a newborn baby. She knew that God had something to tell her. She joined the rest of the session, waiting for God. At the end of the seminar, Yoone shared her testimony with others:

The first day of the seminar, I decided to commit suicide. So I called my family and friend. The seminar was my last hope. But after the first session, I felt like this was not for me. I felt like God abandoned me so that I was possessed by a demon.
The only way was to die. I didn't have any option. As soon as I decided to kill myself, I somehow started to miss my people. So I called everyone close to me except my mom. I didn't intend to, but I just didn't.
Yesterday, on the second day of the seminar, I remembered something. It was an incident when I was three years old. It was not the first time I remembered it, but I didn't take it seriously before.
Yesterday, during the small group session, there was a story shared by a lady from my group. It was about her relations with her daughter. While I was listening to her story, the incident I recalled earlier came up again. This time, I felt severe pain in my heart, but this time, I think I began

to understand why. It gave me a clue to the question that I have always wondered about: Why is this young girl crying inside me. Finally, I found out why.

This realization gave me a whole new perspective. I know it sounds weird, but now I understand everything. I found the answer. It is so clear.

I was the second child in my family. My grandma didn't like me because I was a girl and not a boy as she had expected. She was mean to my mom because she wanted to have a grandson. I cried a lot, and it didn't help. My grandma called me a pain in the ass. She often told my family that I was the one who had ruined the family. Even when she had Alzheimer's, she still remembered me as a pain in the ass. It was just what my family had called me since I was born.

The memory that I recounted earlier happened when I was three years old. It was the day my father had a trial. My family was worried and nervous. I remember that something made me cry, and I couldn't stop. So my grandma was upset, saying I was bringing bad luck to the family. She took me outside the house and left me on the muddy road. It was raining hard that day. It was only when I was about to pass out in the muddy water that my family brought me inside.

As I vividly remember the incident, I began to understand the deep sorrow inside me. It was because of my mom. I expected my mom to protect me when grandma left me on the muddy street on that rainy day. But my mom left me instead. Since that day, loneliness and heartache have stayed in my mind for the past twenty years. My mom abandoned me, and I didn't have a "home." This is why I have been wandering around looking for someone to love me.

Eventually, I met my boyfriend, who loved me, but when we broke up, I started to see this little girl crying inside me again. I really thought I had a mental illness. Now I know it is me crying for mom on that muddy road. I deeply wanted to receive love from my mom. I have tried to be a good daughter, hoping Mom would love me, but she didn't.

Whenever mom goes to fortune tellers, they would say I am the one who ruins the family. They would even say it was because of my religion. I am the only Christian member in my family. My mom had never shown that she liked me, and I thought it was because of grandma, who called me a pain in the ass. Sometimes, even my dad told me that what grandma said was true. So I couldn't stay at home. When I first had a seizure, I just came from the house of a friend whom I met at church. I came home late, and mom wanted to talk with me.

"What is wrong with you? We need to talk."

She sounded nice and calm. It was very different from usual, and it made me confused. I didn't know how to react when she talked to me that nicely, for I was only used to her shouting at me with her mean voice.

I have always wanted to have a nice talk with my mom,

but when she finally asked me to have a talk with a calming voice, I wasn't happy. Instead, I was confused. I didn't know what to say. I told her that I was moving out. My mom had this scary look and said the harsh words she used to say. At that moment, I think I had lost my mind. I told her terrible things. I cried and screamed like a monster until I passed out. When I woke up, my family told me what I was like, and I was convinced that I was really possessed by a demon.

So my mom took me to a psychiatrist. She also took me to a pastor, who told me I was possessed by a demon. He prayed for me. After three days of special "treatment," he told me that the demon was gone and that I would find my peace. However, I felt more miserable than before and thought God had abandoned me. I desperately want to believe that God loves me, but I have always felt alone in the darkness.

When I was in college, I joined a Christian club. I wanted to feel God's love. Whenever I asked for love, what I had was coldness and loneliness. I felt like God also rejected me, and I wanted to kill myself.

Yesterday, while I was praying, God showed me the scene when I was three years old—the one that kept replaying in my mind. I was crying on the muddy road. When this scene came up, I screamed because I felt so much pain in my heart. But then I think God "spoke" to me, telling me that I needed to forgive my mom. So I started to pray for her, and I felt the pain disappear. For the first time, I felt God's love. My heart was always so cold, but it became so warm. Suddenly, that little girl crying inside me disappeared. Since then, I have been trembling. I am pleased, but at the same time, I am shocked. I can't believe that God knew I was left on the muddy road by myself and crying. This made me tremble.

Since then, all the symptoms that Yoone has - both physically and psychologically - disappeared. What happened to Yoone? How can both body and mind heal in such a short time?

God reminded Yoone of the incident that gave her deep sorrow. More importantly, God helped Yoone realize that he knew about it, and this made her feel secure about being herself. This incident convinced Yoone to believe in God's love.

A finger infection due to a splinter can only be treated by removing the splinter from the finger. Likewise, diseases of the body and mind can only be healed by removing the source that causes them.

Yoone was ill, and her mind was weaker than her body. She even passed out due to the "pain" she was harboring inside. However, as no one knew the cause that gave her such pain, no one could help her.

We can easily remove a splinter from a finger because we can see it. However, if we have one in our internal organs, we need a surgeon. If a "splinter" is in our heart where a CAT scan can't show, who can remove it for us?

This book shares actual stories in which the Holy Spirit removed such "splinters" from people's hearts. The Holy Spirit healed a deep wound in these people's hearts. This book explains the biblical grounds of these cases and the key to the Gospel.

We suggest that you allow your heart to follow this book. You can be assured that you will have the same healing experience shared in this book and in the offline seminar. Such an experience comes from the grace and power of the Holy Spirit.

A theoretical basis for Biblical Inner Healing and counseling: The New Covenant Model

The Biblical Inner Healing Ministry Center[1] developed the New Covenant Model. This model is based on the new covenant principle, which is the Gospel of the New Testament. The Biblical Inner Healing Ministry Center operates all of its ministry and education activities based on this principle.

---

[1] In 2003, the Biblical Inner Healing Ministry Center was established. The Center has led the inner healing ministry in Korea with regularly held three-day seminars here and abroad, counseling center, publications, prison and youth ministries, addiction ministries, programs with the government, and so on.

1. What is the New Covenant Model?

The new covenant model is the healing principle and model based on the new covenant. This new covenant, prophesied in the Old Testament,[2] was guaranteed by Jesus Christ at his last holy communion.[3] In other words, it refers to the entire ministry under the governance of Jesus Christ.

In referring to the new covenant model, Biblical Inner Healing primarily focuses on healing inside people. This healing is revealed through the Holy Spirit by engraving the words of God in human hearts with the love of Jesus Christ who died at the Cross.

The word "testament" in the Old and New Testaments refers to "conviction" or "consent." The former refers to God's conviction for human salvation, while the latter refers to God's consent for human salvation after Christ.[4]

We can find God's conviction from the Old Testament and the consent of grace from Jesus from the New Testament. These two testaments share the same purpose: salvation. However, there is a critical difference between them in the path to and the content of such salvation. The Old Testament prophesies the Gospel by the grace of the New Testament, while the New Testament emphasizes the significance of the new covenant based on the Old Testament. Getting to know what the new covenant means has the

---

[2] Ezekiel 36:25-27; Jeremiah 31:33-34

[3] Luke 22:19-20

[4] Mears, Henrietta C. (1997) *What the Bible is All About*. Royal Regal Books.

power to change all kinds of issues, including the salvation and sanctification that Christians have.

Malcolm Smith[5] said that Jesus's last holy communion was the supper to state the enactment of the new covenant. He defined "the new testament in my blood" as the new, legitimate covenant "as it is validated with my blood."

The New Covenant Model focuses on the change that occurs when the Holy Spirit renews an individual's core belief system. This change, however, doesn't happen due to the efforts of humans alone in keeping the commandments. Rather, this renewal occurs when we focus on God and our relations with him.

Christianity sees the core of healing within the human belief system that is shaped by sin. Its primary focus is not the cause of one's inner wounds. However, there has been a lack of effort in applying this principle to the counseling model applied in Christianity. Thus, the New Covenant Model introduced in this book was developed to apply this core principle to the process of inner healing.

The link that connects God to his people is based on the covenant.[6] However, human disobedience led to the destruction of the first covenant[7], resulting in complete

---

[5] Smith, Malcolm (2002) *The Lost Secret of the New Covenant.* Harrison House.

[6] Exodus 34:27; Leviticus 26:42; 2 Kings 23:3

[7] Hebrews 8:9

despair.⁸ The apostle Paul said that the disobedience that destroyed the first covenant remained among Christians, continuing to create confusion and psychological despair.⁹

The New Covenant Model believes that those who remain confused and in despair require counseling and healing. As stated by the apostle Paul, there's an inherent weakness and vulnerability in Christians who are too weak to defeat sin. This weakness brings despair and guilt.[10] The good news is that Paul has found a surprising secret to turn this great despair around: He found the new covenant enacted by Jesus Christ.[11]

How can complete despair turn into victory? This does not rely on human effort. There is another power based on this biblical principle, and the New Covenant Model offers materialized practical steps to achieve counseling and healing.

2. The New Covenant Model and the healing process

In defining a sinner, the New Covenant Model believes that status matters and not behavior. This approach implies

---

[8] Adam and Eve broke the promise they made to God. Cain sinned regardless of God's word to rule over the sin.(Genesis 4:7) All the commitments that Moses made with God were also broken. The apostle Paul said, "There is no one righteous, not even one; there is no one who understands; there is no one who seeks God. All have turned away, they have together become worthless; there is no one who does good, not even one." (Romans 3:10–12)

[9] Romans 7:18–19

[10] Romans 7

[11] Romans 8:1–2

that humans cannot learn how to avoid sin.[12]

The only way to change a man is to implant a new life through Jesus Christ. When we are born again through the life of Jesus Christ, our status and nature are entirely renewed. However, regardless of this significant change, our brain doesn't completely understand what has happened. So we are still covered by our past understandings of the world.[13] This is where Satan works. Satan uses our lack of understanding and our bodies that are used to doing things from the past. Thus, even though our spirit has been born again, we remain immature because of our old habits. Satan knows this weakness and tells lies to manipulate us.

The New Covenant Model is designed to intervene and help us understand the new status given by Jesus. It lets us know of our old thinking habits and heals the sorrows from our old experiences and relations.

On the one hand, it is ironic that more guilt follows when Christians intentionally exert efforts to make changes to their old mindset. This can be described as a vicious cycle experienced by Christians. On the other hand, while motivation leads to condemnation, it also leads to rededication. Steve Macvey said that the only way to break this vicious cycle is to understand the procedure of the new covenant.[14]

---

[12] Gillham, Bill (1993) *Lifetime guarantee*. Harvest House Publishers.
[13] Ibid.
[14] McVey, Steve (1995) *Grace Walk*. Harvest House Publishers.

The New Covenant Model

```
NEW BEING FOR  ←----  NEW LIFE THROUGH  ----→  SINNER
NEW LIFE              JESUS CHRIST
     ↓
┌─────────────── Having a New Mindset ───────────────┐
│  Internal belief → Writing God's → Changes in → Intimate  │
│  system            rule on mind    feeling,      relations with │
│                                    mind,         Christ    │
│                                    practice               │
└───────────────────────────────────────────────────┘
                                                    ↓
WORLD OF GOD  ←----  IMPACT ON       ----→  FOLLOWING
                     CHRISTIAN              THE RULES
                     COMMUNITY
```

The approach of the New Covenant Model brings significant spiritual changes to Christians and leads to healing of the body and the mind. It is grace that allows us to know and believe in our new status, and this happens when our relationship with God grows. Having a mature relationship with God leads to changes in our behaviors. Then, our behaviors follow our commitments. When we genuinely believe in our new status, we see ourselves as a family of God, not just an independent being with our own bodies and lives. In this aspect, the outcome of the healing and growth achieved through the New Covenant Model impacts personal salvation, in particular, and the Christian community in general. In other words, it has the power to change our lives by having an impact on ourselves and the community. At the same time, the community can help individual Christians achieve this change.

Ban said that the principle of Christian counseling is to

help counselees believe that God is good. This will lead to more religious experiences and a renewed conception of religion, not for self-interest, but for God's purpose. It will help counselees become more engaged in their communities and churches, where they can gain further social support and encouragement.[15] The New Covenant Model also shares this idea.

3. The New Covenant vs. The Old Covenant

What is different between the two?

1) Changes in the system that bring holiness

On the one hand, the Old Covenant says that obeying the rules from God leads us to holiness and becoming God's people. In this respect, good Christians are those who obey God's rules. On the other hand, the New Covenant says that we need to be born again through Jesus Christ to be holy and to become God's people.[16]

Gillham stated that it is not our behavior that determines our nature; rather, being born determines our nature. While people focus on behavior in defining sin, God doesn't.

The New Covenant emphasizes that the way to be holy is to acknowledge, receive, and focus on our new status in

---

[15] Ban, Shin Hwan (2005). "Based on the analysis on the relation between the depression and religion." *Korean Christian Counselling Review* (In Korean).

[16] Hebrews 9, Jeremiah 32:38–41

Christ that is given to us.[17]

There is not even one person but Jesus, who is right with God and follows the Old Covenant.[18]

When viewed another way, the Old Covenant failed to lead us to be holy because if there was nothing wrong with it, then we would not have needed a New Covenant.[19] Such a failure, however, is not due to its content, but the corrupted mind of a human. Our corrupted minds have made it impossible to follow the Old Covenant, which is why we need the New Covenant to turn us into a whole new package, regardless of our corrupted minds.[20]

---

[17] Gillham, Bill (1993) *Lifetime guarantee*. Harvest House Publishers.

[18] Romans 3:10

[19] Hebrews 8:7

[20] Hebrews 8:8–13

What does the Bible say?

Old Covenant	New Covenant
It was written on stone	It is written deep inside people
2 Corinthians 3:3	2 Corinthians 3:3
It is about rules that bring death	It comes from God's spirit. It brings a new life to people
2 Corinthians 3:6	2 Corinthians 3:6; 17
It shows people are guilty	It brings righteousness
2 Corinthians 3:9	2 Corinthians 3:9
It came to an end	It lasts
2 Corinthians 3:11	2 Corinthians 3:11
Moses' face did not continue to be bright with the light from God. So he covered his face	When a person turns to the Lord, then God takes away the veil
2 Corinthians 3:13	2 Corinthians 3:16; 18
It came to an end	It lasts and shows the power of God, which is ever-increasing
2 Corinthians 3:11	2 Corinthians 3:18

2) Rule of God written on a piece of stone vs. Deep inside our minds

In the Old Covenant, the rule of God was written on a piece of stone. In people's minds, something other than the rule of God is written. Therefore, people could pretend to follow the rules but couldn't live with them. It is true that the words written inside us always have more power to control us than those written on a piece of stone.

However, the New Covenant says that this time, God promised to write his rules deep inside our minds and not on the piece of stone. This leads us to become right with God.[21] Marshall explained this change as follows:[22]

"God resolved people's disobedience by writing the rule not on a piece of stone but deep inside of their minds. Now, people can follow the rule of God internally, not externally. When God's words internally work inside of people, their corrupted mind becomes something new. The mind becomes free from sins. This allows for a new mindset that harmonizes the new internal rule. The Old Covenant was the rule written on a piece of stone that hid sin. On the other hand, the New Covenant is the internal rule in our mind that washes sin."

---

[21] Romans 8:4

[22] Marshall, Tom (2001) *Living in the Freedom of the Spirit.* Sovereign World Ltd.

SESSION 1

WHAT IS BIBLICAL INNERHEALING?

Why do we need healing in our subconsciousness?
What happens when we are broken and hurt?
What are the symptoms?
Who can heal the subconsciousness of our minds?

PURPOSE OF THE SESSION

To know ourselves, we need to know what fills our minds. By exploring memories and feelings from our past experiences, we can answer the question of who we are.

Knowing ourselves allows us to know God. Knowing God allows us to identify ourselves in the view of God. Related to this, Biblical Inner Healing is the procedure for knowing ourselves in the view of God.

WHAT IS BIBLICAL INNER HEALING?

1. Inward man: Two different meanings

The word inward in the Bible implies two different meanings. Biblical Inner Healing refers to the first meaning of inward.

First, it means the inside of a human's mind, which can be distinguished from one's physical body.

> *Therefore we do not lose heart.*
> *Though outwardly, we are wasting away, yet inwardly we are being renewed day by day.*
> *2 Corinthians 4:16*

Several expressions in the Bible refer to the meaning of the inside of humans that cannot be seen. The following are some examples:

- **Inner self:** Peter asked to keep our inner selves as the unfading beauty of a gentle and quiet spirit (1 Peter 3:4)
- **Ship:** Apostle Paul warned about worshiping a ship. Jesus said that whoever believes in him will have rivers of living water flowing from within them. Lawrence Crabb describes the ship as a metaphor, which implies the inner part of our identities that is eager to be filled.
- **Center of the heart:** 1 Samuel 16:7; Psalms 51:6
- **Heart:** Proverbs 14:10

Second, the word inward is also used to refer to the inner self within our mind that receives Jesus Christ.

For in my inner being I delight in God's law
Romans 7:22

Paul used the term "old self" to describe one's status before receiving Jesus Christ.

For we know that our old self was crucified with him
so that the body ruled by sin might be done away
with, that we should no longer be slaves to sin
Romans 6:6

2. The inner self in Biblical Inner Healing

In Biblical Inner Healing, we use the terms inner self or inward to imply the first meaning of inward, not the latter.

The word "inward" in this book implies the inside of our mind that is different from our physical exterior.

Thus, the latter meaning of inward is not appropriate when related to the word healing because when it is used to refer to an inner being who receives Jesus Christ, it would mean a complete being who no longer needs any form of healing.

Therefore, in reading this book, please note that the inward or inner self refers to your mind that is distinct from our external physical body.

Not all Christians have a healthy, mature inner self. Our inner selves can still be vulnerable to sin. Therefore, we need to take care of our inner selves. In Ephesians 3:16, the Apostle Paul prayed with all his heart for people to have strengthened inner selves through the power of the Holy Spirit.

Biblical Inner Healing is a procedure in which the Holy Spirit heals and changes the hearts of God's children. It also refers to the spiritual journey based on the words of God, who promised to heal our hearts. Here, we study those words and rules of God, apply them to actual cases, and believe the Holy Spirit can strengthen the entire healing procedure.

Christians are on an ongoing journey to be like Jesus Christ. However, for this journey, we need healing in our inner selves, and to achieve this, we need to take care of past memories and feelings. At this point, we may wonder, "How do our memories impact our minds, our inner selves?"

The human brain saves every experience we have. It is like a supercomputer. We may forget past experiences, but this doesn't mean that our brain has completely deleted them. For example, our brain moves memories to a different area called "oblivion." Thus, these memories are still in us, even though we may forget them.

Generally, we can remember direct and indirect experiences. As time goes by, these experiences become memories, some of which move to a deeper level and are placed deep inside our subconscious. In keeping the memories, your brain retains details of what happened and how we felt at that time. Therefore, when you have a traumatic experience, your brain keeps memories of both the experience and the accompanying pain. You may forget, but your brain keeps both of them in your subconscious.

The issue is that some traumatic memories infect other parts of your mind. Much like a virus creates mutant strains, traumatic memories also create such variants. These variants "infect" our current lives. While we don't recognize or remember it, our past is firmly attached to the present. Thus, current issues can never be solved unless we fix past issues in our memories, as the following figure shows.

When we see bushes, as in the figure, we try to cut them off and remove them. This effort includes all the moral and religious efforts one has made. However, no matter how we try, the bushes will always be there unless we cut out the roots under the ground.

The Holy Spirit knows how crucial it is to cut out the root that nurtures bitterness. It fundamentally wants to remove the seed that raises the *bitter root*, which is often found in the deepest place of our minds: the subconscious.

Figure 1

In the figure, the arrow implies the specific experiences from the past that shaped our personality, while the underground refers to our minds. The seed is the interpretation of past experiences from our own perspective. The roots coming from the seed are bitter roots that distort the truth and lead to adverse emotions. The bushes on the ground come from the bitter root. This bush implies unhealthy personalities or habits stemming from bitter roots that hurt other people.

3. Do Christians, with the Holy Spirit in their minds, also need healing in their subconsciousness?

When we become Christians, do all the hurts and issues in

our minds disappear? Some would answer "Yes" and say that the past doesn't have any power, as the Bible said it is a new creation if anyone is in Christ. However, in our lives, we know that the answer is actually "No."

Sell saw many Christians believe that "Pains from childhood don't affect my life as I received Jesus Christ." However, Sell also realized that there was no significant change, even after he became Christian. He didn't become spiritually mature. His weakness was still there.[23]

At the same time, some Christian leaders emphasized that there cannot be any issues in our minds if we really receive Jesus Christ. While this sounds good, it has also confused many Christians, who put their efforts into following God's word, especially when they have adverse emotions. This has planted doubts about their identity as good Christians and has also brought guilt and despair.

As Christians also need healing in their subconsciousness, it doesn't mean that the grace and power of the Cross are not enough. Instead, experiencing the healing in our minds by the Holy Spirit is the key step to believing God is the one who created us.

Christians are new creations who are no longer related to the past. Therefore, we need to clean our mess from the past. Just neglecting painful memories from the past doesn't set us free from it. Inner healing is necessary. It is not, however, about revisiting past experiences but a

---

[23] Sell, Charles (1989) *Unfinished Business*. Multnomah Books.

procedure that sets us free from the past in a healthy way that allows us to be wholly united with Christ. The subconscious is the storage that keeps all those memories from the past. Even though we lock it and don't visit, these memories are still inside us.[24]

Without the help of the Holy Spirit, we can never see all the pains and wounds deep inside our subconsciousness. Sometimes, people use psychological defensive systems, such as denial or repression, so that they don't have to face painful memories. However, this is like pushing an air-filled balloon into the water. As the water pushes the balloon back when your power becomes weak, it brings massive confusion into your lives.

Other times, we try to hide the wounds in our hearts, but in the end, everything we tried to hide would come outside and take control of our minds. We can't think right. Our spirit is in pain, as it can't connect with God. Thus, inner healing is the key to the healing of our subconsciousness.[25]

4. The consequences of a wounded heart

The wounded heart can be hidden. However, no one can avoid its impact on one's life. The following are the consequences of a wounded heart.

---

[24] Ibid.

[25] Torrey, Reuben A (2013) *The Real Christ*. Whitaker House.

Difficulties in relationships with others

This is the most frequent symptom found in people with wounded hearts. They often show two features: they are either too dependent on others or they always want to have control over others.

On the one hand, there are dependent people. They adopt the opinions and thoughts of their parents as their own. When they grow up, they adopt the opinions of friends, partners, and spouses as their own. They show an extremely passive lifestyle. What happens when people with such passivity are disappointed with someone they depend on? For example, their spouse? They face extreme despair that collapses their lives. They need to find another person on whom they can depend. At the same time, ironically, they won't be able to trust the new person on whom they will depend.

On the other hand, some people feel secure only when they control others and everyday matters. They act like dictators. If, for example, a father is obsessed over controlling every family member who has to follow only his opinion, the father would feel disrespected when his children express other opinions.

Arrogance

Being arrogant is different from being confident. Arrogant people are critical and tend to judge others. When someone seems better than them, they find a flaw to humiliate them. When someone seems weaker than them, they ignore them and look down on them.

Negative words and mindset

These kinds of people often blame parents, others, or society for everything. So they always bear a grudge against someone. They also feel resentment toward God. This kind of grudge inside people can eventually transform into outright hostility.

Depression and obsessive-compulsive personality

Individuals with this kind of personality don't have energy in their lives due to depression. An obsessive personality weakens their nerves. Moreover, being nervous and obsessive leads to feelings of guilt. The Bible tells how the guilty makes people distressed (Psalms 32:3–4).

Lack of conviction in God's love

As they harbor distorted perceptions, they can't see God accurately. They can pretend and say the right things about God. However, what they may really believe is the wrong image of God, thinking:
"God is unpredictable. He is fickle."
"God is cruel. He enjoys giving pain to people. He just

watches me when I am in pain."
"He is always unhappy with me."
"He is tired of me, who consistently fails."
"They always have this negative, wrong image of God. It impacts their spiritual stability."

Fluctuation and depression in spiritual life

As they lack conviction in God's love, their faith fluctuates depending on the circumstances. Regardless of their long years of faith as Christians, when they face difficulties in their lives, they will immediately doubt God's love and presence.

5. Our past shapes our personalities. To change our personalities, we need to heal our past

Different from temperament,[26] our personalities are shaped by experiences. It is not given by God. It is the result of a wounded heart and the act of sinning.

Therefore, our hearts can be and must be healed. Our personality can be renewed in God through the Holy Spirit and his love. We're responsible for the decision to keep the old, sinful personality, even after becoming a Christian. It is

---

[26] Personality and temperament are not the same. "Temperament" refers to the foundation of the personality given at birth. It is not based on experiences but on natural traits. On the other hand, "personality" includes acquired traits through experiences. Chung, Chung Suk (1995) *Samo rel we han sang dam (Counseling for ministers' wives)* Bedani (In Korean).

like keeping a snake in the house. We have to get rid of it so that we can fix the unhealthy areas in our personalities.

> *It will be as though a man fled from a lion only to meet a bear, as though he entered his house and rested his hand on the wall only to have a snake bite him.*
> *Amos 5:19*

Our personalities bring outcomes to our lives. Therefore, memories that keep old personalities must be fixed. This is because bad memories become more robust if we try to let them out. They are revealed through our personalities. They hide deep inside our consciousness and come up in the form of disease, marital issues, and spiritual despair. Thus, it is crucial to find and heal the memories that have shaped our old personalities.[27]

J. E. Adams also said that it is crucial to review our past to understand current issues. In this sense, exploring the past involves reviewing the cause of our current behaviors.

6. How can we heal from past memories and renew our personalities?

The fact is that we can't change past memories and old personalities by ourselves. Hypnosis, counseling, and psychotherapy cannot be the answer. Only God can do the job.

---

[27] Seamands, David A. (1985) *Healing of Memories*. Christian Press.

Here are the reasons why:

Humans cannot see their subconsciousness by themselves. Subconsciousness starts before birth and has all those memories that we cannot remember. However, God knows every detail of these memories (Psalms 139:1–4).

Psalms 139 shows the following image of God: God created us. God was there before us. God knew our future, even before we were born. As he knows everything, including our past, he knows exactly what made us hurt, disappointed, and sad. Even the darkness can't be hidden from him. He knows everything deep inside our minds and sees the seeds of bitter roots. At the same time, he is the one who can renew our painful memories.

In our subconsciousness, sinful personalities or thoughts are inherited from our parents. These are originated from the original sins of Adam and Eve, and only Jesus Christ can handle this issue (John 1:12).

We can see a case in which family members share similar sinful behaviors. It is also found in the Bible.[28] Some people treat the story of Adam and Eve as a myth and be-

---

[28] Isaac showed the sins and mistakes of Abraham. Abraham lied that his wife was his sister for his sake (Genesis 12:13). Isaac also did the same as his father (Genesis 26:7).

lieve Adam and Eve are unrelated to them. However, the behaviors of Adam and Eve are still reflected in us, even to this day.[29]

If our sinful behavior is inherited from our parents, how can we be free from it? The only way is through Jesus Christ. By receiving Jesus, we can be officially free from all our "inherited" sins. However, this process of cutting off old habits requires our efforts. In particular, we need to use God's words to cut off our old habits.

Without God, we can still find out what is inside our subconsciousness. However, no one can heal it, except God. We have to know what is in us to heal. Unfortunately, even though we find out the cause that brings pain in the present, we can't go back or fix the past. However, God can.

People have used various measures to get away from the past. In 1953, scientists found that cutting off some parts of a chimpanzee's brain reduced its rowdiness. Surgeons applied the procedure to humans. Between 1955 and 1975, about 70,000 patients underwent surgery. Surgeons cut parts of their frontal lobes that trigger the tendency for rowdiness. However, the surgery patients experienced severe side effects. Today, no one does the surgery anymore. Unfortunately, no one has compensated for the lives of pa-

---

[29] Adam and Eve followed what they wanted instead of God's word. This is selfishness. Today, humans tend to practice the same selfishness as Adam and Eve and commit all kinds of sins. Murder, lying, using others for self-interest, disobeying God, and worshiping idols are all due to selfishness.

tients who underwent surgery.[30]

Figure 2

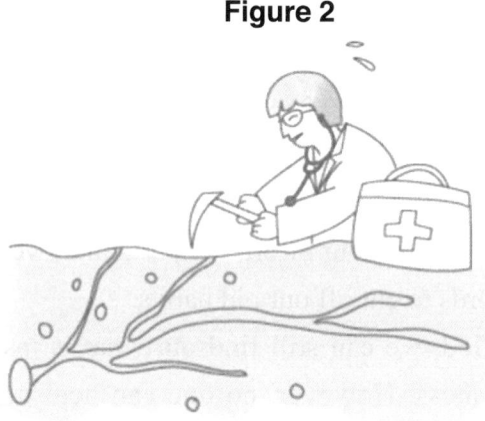

In the figure, the ground shows the inside of a patient's heart. The seeds refer to the past that harms the patient's current life. A doctor uses a shovel to look into the ground and find the cause that impacts the patient's current life.

Removing the past memory does not remove the wounds in our hearts caused by the past memory. To remove the wounds in our hearts from the past, there's no way to achieve this, but through God. It is God who can heal the past.

God cuts off the channel that connects our hearts to the past. God has promised that he would set us free from the past and rid us of our guilt and regrets.

---

[30] Collins, Gary (1980) *Christian counseling: a comprehensive guide*. Word Books.

7. There is hope, as Jesus said that he will heal us

While he was still in human form, Jesus had shown several miracles to heal people. It clearly shows how he thinks about illness in our bodies and minds. He wants our minds and bodies to be well.

> *On hearing this, Jesus said, "It is not the healthy who need a doctor, but the sick. But go and learn what this means: 'I desire mercy, not sacrifice.' For I have not come to call the righteous, but sinners."*
> *Matthew 9:12-13*

> *But he was pierced for our transgressions, he was crushed for our iniquities; the punishment that brought us peace was on him, and by his wounds we are healed.*
> *Isaiah 53:5*

As a healer, Jesus wants to heal us, including our hearts and bodies. The Holy Spirit exercises Jesus's word in us. Jesus completed all to heal us. More importantly, anyone with a disease can ask Jesus for healing.

He knows that our hearts are broken. He said our hearts are imprisoned and locked up in a prison of fears. It can be more painful than being behind bars physically. Yet, Jesus said he came to us to set us free (Isaiah 61:1–3).

8. Read and follow this book, and the Holy Spirit will heal your wounded heart

First of all, you must let go of your ego and confidence that you already know everything about yourself. Pray and ask God if there's anything in your heart that he wants to heal. There's no one who does not need healing from God.

CASE

God found and came to me, hiding in a barley field

"I didn't know anything about this Biblical Inner Healing(BIH) seminar. I just came with my friend. At the end of the year, I go to the prayer house. Next year, I will play a serious role in the church. So I thought, why not, I can spend more time praying to prepare myself."

She was in her early fifties. She looked like a nice lady, whom we see in a church.

"In the first session, I was listening to the purpose of the BIH seminar, and I was assured that it was God who brought me here."

"How come you had that assurance in the introduction session?" I asked.

"I have had an anger issue. I don't get mad at others but at my family. Especially, I am always furious with my husband. I tried so many things to deal with this anger issue. I fasted. I prayed to defeat demonic powers. But none of them solved the issue. So I gave up and thought it was just my nature that I couldn't fix. But sometimes, when I get so mad, I can't even pray for days. It takes me so much time to be calm and pray again."

"I see many people with anger issues. On what occasion do you get mad?"

"I don't get mad, in general. But when my husband drinks, I become furious."

"So, does your husband have a drinking problem?"

"No. He doesn't. He never causes any trouble when he drinks, but I cannot bear the fact that he drinks. Whenever I see him drinking, I become furious that I lose control. So I begged him not to drink, but he doesn't get me. He doesn't understand why I'm so mad. So during the session, I realized that it is me who needs to be healed. So I started to pray to know the seed inside me that caused the anger issue."

She started to have a sad look on her face and shared her story:

I was praying, and I remembered an unpleasant experience from the past. You said to keep the focus on God, not on memories. So I asked him again. 'God, why am I always mad at my husband?'

And one memory just popped up. This happened when I was in elementary school. I was doing my homework in the living room, and my dad, drunken, walked in with a shovel. He shouted at me, saying he was going to kill me. I was terrified. I ran to a barley field at the back of my house. I was holding a pencil and eraser. I was so scared that I just ran away with them. I hid in a barley field and watched him scream. I felt like I could die, and I wanted people to know it was me when they found my body. So I tried to write my name on my thigh with a pencil.

Since then, I sometimes remember this incident, but I don't take it seriously. But today, when I remembered this incident while I was praying, I knew it was God who showed me this memory, allowing me to understand why I was furious about my husband's drinking.

It was because of my drunken father who came to kill me. It was not because of my husband. I didn't know. I blamed him for the past years. This seed in my heart made me go through all that suffering even when I am in my fifties.

I was overwhelmed, so I asked to have a one-on-one session. I prayed with a counselor and felt that God had found me in the barley field. He came to me in the barley field. And he told me,

"Your father makes you terrified, but I am your father who doesn't scare you."

When I heard this, I was overwhelmed. I screamed. I don't remember what I said. It is not enough to say, "Thank you, Lord."

The next day, she gave a testimony:

I have been a Christian for the past years, but I have always felt some fear when I think about God. I always say, 'God is good,' but I actually thought of him as a scary god, not a nice one. Now, I know why I had this scary image of God. Deep inside my heart, I had the image of my father coming to kill me. It affected me in the way that I harbored the wrong image of God.

Now, I believe God is good. He's nice. I feel so free. Something weighty disappeared in my heart. I didn't even know I had it. Now, I can't imagine life holding it again.

CASE

Please let me die or allow me to divorce him

I always had the same prayer. Everyone in the neighborhood knew that my husband was an alcoholic. I quit praying about his drinking issue because it didn't work. So I asked God to either allow me to divorce him or die.

Since we married, he has failed to become a breadwinner. He was always out, and when he was home, he was either drunk or sleeping. There were times when he didn't come home for a couple of years, not telling me. I didn't think of him as a husband. I was determined to divorce him when the children became older.

I hated my husband, but as a Christian, I felt guilty. My life was in pain. People always wondered how I managed to stay with him. I didn't know what to do but swallow the pain.

During the session at the BIH seminar, I started to think I could be the one who has issues. I was still mad thinking about my husband, but I asked God. 'God, please tell me what I did wrong!'

I thought that the only fault I had was being a fool and deciding to stay with my husband. However, God reminded me of an unexpected memory. It happened during the Korean war. I saw an image of my father. I was very young. I was sitting in the living room, and there was heavy bombing outside. My father ran away by himself and left me alone in the house. Fortunately, the bombing destroyed all the neighboring houses, except ours. So now I am still alive. I couldn't understand why the memory came to my mind. I had never thought about this before. As I started to think about the incident, tremendous rage surged through me. 'How could he...! How could he...'

I felt extreme anger that I found it hard to breathe. I couldn't sit and listen to the session. I left the building. I looked at the sky and mountains to calm down. However, the extreme anger in my mind wouldn't go away. Soon after, I thought about forgiveness. However, I didn't think I could do it. I was thinking to myself, 'How could he leave that little child and run away?' Then, this image of Jesus on the Cross came to my mind, and it spoke to me.

"I know your father left you, but I was there protecting you. That's why you were safe. So forgive your father."

It was the word of God that I could not rebel. I saw the image of God holding me in his arms when my father left me during that day. I thought to myself, 'Oh, that's why I was safe. At that time, I didn't go to church or believe in

God, but he was protecting me.'

Looking at God holding me, I forgave my father, and I forgave people who have hurt me. I forgave everyone who came to my mind. I started to understand why I hated my husband and why my husband had to drink.

When I was just married, my in-laws put me in an embarrassing situation due to marriage expenses. I wanted my husband to stand up for me, but he didn't. It was the time when I shut him out. I saw a parallel situation between my father and my husband. Neither of them didn't protect me when I was in need. For the first time, I realized that this was why I hated my husband. I cried and cried throughout the seminar. When I came back home, I told my husband.

"It hasn't been easy for me. But now I know that it hasn't been easy for you too."

It was the first time I said these words to my husband. He seemed surprised. He told me in an awkward tone.

"No... honey, I know you had a more difficult time than I had."

It was the first time my husband called me 'honey.' He always called me 'you' or used swear words.

Since then, my family has changed. It's amazing. First, my husband decided to stop drinking. He has been trying so hard that I feel sorry for him. Before, he couldn't stand an hour without drinking. I did everything to stop him from dirking, but none of them worked.

I told him, "Honey, you don't have to be too harsh on

you. You can drink when you want. And ask God to help you."

I was surprised when I realized that I could say such kind words to my husband.

Before, I was full of anger and grudge. I just waited for the day that I would die. Now, my husband, the famous alcoholic in the neighborhood, is changing. I am about to reach my 60th birthday. It is a miracle to have this new life at this time.

CASE

God wiped off the food waste on my body

My mother is in her nineties, and she recently received Jesus. I have spent so many years trying to make her believe in God. I always thought she was so stubborn that I couldn't let her. Now, I know it was my fault. The changes I experienced allowed me to help my mother receive Jesus.

I have a secret that I haven't told anyone. As I became a minister, this secret grew bigger in me. So I need to share this with others so that I can feel relieved.

I have this vision that comes to my mind from time to time. In the vision, someone is ruining dinner by continuously throwing broken dinner plates. The shards are so sharp, and I feel frightened that they may hurt someone really bad. I didn't understand why I had this vision in my mind. I thought about demon possession. I prayed, but it didn't go away. Whenever I had this vision, I remember what my father used to say:

"Take care of your plate unless it will bring you bad luck."

My life has been very tough. My children died. So did my husband. When my husband passed away, I was left with my young girls. I assumed that this vision was a warning that I was going to have bad luck.

So I worked hard and tried to be a good Christian. However, this terrifying vision wouldn't go away. Sometimes, I would be sitting at the dining table and feel a strong urge to throw plates and forks. During those times, I really thought a demon was sitting next to me at the dining table. I haven't shared this story with anyone before. I was afraid of what people would think because I am a preacher. Even though I faced so many hardships in my life, I didn't cry. But when I came to the seminar, I didn't know why, but I cried and cried, and I even remembered one incident from the past.

I was very young, and I was sitting on my mom's lap. She was eating dinner. My father was in another room, eating his dinner. They were in different rooms but were talking about something. Suddenly, my father threw his plate at my mom. My mom threw back her fork to my father. In the middle of this, I saw myself sitting on my mom's lap, also eating my dinner. I wasn't wearing anything. My parents were throwing plates and fighting, and my body was covered with food waste that they threw at each other.

I realized this was what actually happened in the vision

that has horrified me! It was not a demonic obsession. I was not crazy. This was something that actually happened! But...now what can I do about it?

I decided to undergo a one-on-one counseling session. Although I was afraid to share the story even with a counselor because I was a preacher, I wanted to be renewed in God. I was praying with a counselor, and God reminded me of this vision again.

This time, I saw something that I didn't see before. God was sitting in that messy room, also covered with broken plates and food waste. When my parents were fighting, I saw God holding me and taking me to the attic. He wiped off the food waste on my body. When he was with me, I was still mad at my mom because I thought it was my mom who started the fight, but God told me:

"Your mom just doesn't know what to do. Let's give her a break."

And that was it. As soon as I heard God's voice, the deep pain in my heart gradually subsided, and my heart was filled with pure joy. God put me in new clothes, and hand in hand, we walked to some wasteland where plants started to grow. I, a little girl, had so much fun playing with God.

I cried over and over during the counseling. I am almost 50 years old now, but my heart was full of joy, like a little kid holding God's hand. I realized he had held my hand since then. He has always been with me. I have worked as a preacher, but I have never felt his presence this close. He is so close to me, like the air I breathe in.

Since then, I have felt differently about my mom. I miss my mom, and I feel really sorry for her. At her birthday party, I told her to receive Jesus. Before, she wouldn't even let me speak about it. But this time, she just said "Okay," like a little girl. It was a miracle.

I didn't know that I had this huge grudge against my mom. Even though I spoke to her so many times about Jesus, this grudge was there between my mom and me. Now, without the grudge, she hears my words about Jesus. She used to be stubborn, but now she listens to what I say to her.

At the same time, my three daughters became the most reliable colleagues in God. They witnessed everything that I had been going through. Before, when they saw me in pain, they blamed God. But the changes in myself and their grandmother touched their hearts.

"Mom, you are the most respectful person I know. I don't blame God anymore. I see that he is alive. I want to live my life for him."

It makes me feel like I have the whole universe. I am a witness to inner healing. I will carry out the ministry to share the potential of inner healing in God.

SESSION 2

KNOWLEDGE vs. RELATIONSHIP

When you humble yourself before God,
He will lift you up.

There are two fundamentally different ways of living. The second session of the Biblical Inner Healing seminar is about this difference.

The first way of life is the life empowered by one's relationship with God, while the second way is the life empowered by yourself, who left God, as in Genesis 3.

PURPOSE OF THE SESSION

The essential task for God was to have a relationship with us. He wants us to stay in the relationship and reap the fruits from the tree of life. However, we chose the tree of knowledge over God, resulting in us being fooled that such knowledge would make us happy. We became enslaved, pursuing knowledge. This way of life not only set us away from having a relationship with God; it also led us to arrogance.

Unfortunately, many Christians are still pursuing the second way of life. Thus, the aim of this session is to renew ourselves from the latter way of life and seek a life driven by a better relationship with God.

KNOWLEDGE vs. RELATIONSHIP

1. There is an ongoing struggle between the tree of life and knowledge

When people say they know something, it implies two different meanings. First, they know based on their experiences. Second, they know based on the knowledge they possess.

In the Bible, Hebrews distinguish these different meanings of know. The word know in the Bible was translated from the Hebrew word *yaw-dah* (עָדַי). When we say a couple knows each other as they have a relationship, the word yaw-dah is used. When the Bible uses the word know, it refers to "knowing something based on actual experience and relationship."

The relationship gives the power to have personal and spiritual growth.

Suppose you have a broken heart from breaking up with your loved one. In that case, you know that it is a relationship that gives you happiness, not knowledge.

Our inner being must have a relationship before knowledge. When we have a relationship, knowledge follows.

In a sense, newborn babies know their mom without being aware of her age, hometown, etc. Babies can't speak, but they know their mom. This demonstrates how knowing through a relationship works. Conversely, having a Ph.D. degree in God doesn't guarantee that you will believe in God's love.

We think we know "A" if we have knowledge of it. If we accumulate knowledge of God, we believe that we know God.

This is the way of thinking that has been naturally fixed in humans since Genesis.

We can't be certain that we know God, either based on knowledge or relationship. Only God can tell.

This is because we don't acknowledge the difference between them. Moreover, knowledge makes humans arrogant. Pharisees and scribes thought they knew God better than anyone. They were full of knowledge of God. When they met Jesus in person, they didn't recognize him, so they killed him.

Figure 3 [31]

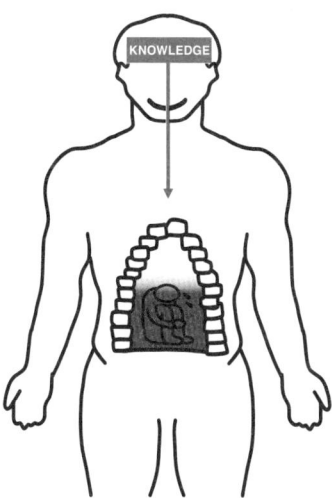

On the one hand, what we know through knowledge doesn't directly impact our inner being. There's a wall between them. The wall blocks knowledge from speaking to our inner being. On the other hand, what we know through relationships can penetrate the wall and speak to our inner being.

God wants us to know him based on relationship, not knowledge.

Knowledge of God can help us when we have a relationship with him.

---

[31] Marshall, Tom (2000) *Free Indeed*. Sovereign World.

However, without the help of the Holy Spirit, knowledge can't do anything by itself. It is just information that cannot help us achieve growth in our inner being.

2. How can we tell that we know God based on relationships, not knowledge?

Knowledge can't change the character and life of a person.

An inner being grows through having a relationship with God, and it changes a person's character. If we have more knowledge, we become more arrogant, and we begin to teach people things that we can't. In this case, knowledge is powerless, like a paper tiger. As one person puts it:

"When I was about to commit suicide, I realized that there's no God inside me. I thought I was a good Christian, knowing him well. But when I faced enormous sorrow inside, I saw there's nobody in me but myself, crying. God wasn't there. I had God only in my head. I didn't have a living God in me."

Informative knowledge can't impact hidden motives.

To see changes in ourselves, we have to let Jesus take the driver's seat in our lives. We are full of knowledge and comfortably seated in the driver's seat. On the outside, it seems we are obeying God's words, but on the inside, as long as we take the driver's seat, we are not listening to him and would rather be the ruler of our lives.

Knowledge is what makes us feel secure. So when someone attacks our knowledge, we take offense and attack back.

We don't attack back, not because we want to honor God's word, but to show our knowledge. When we all have the same goal of keeping God's words, our Christian community can be united in the Holy Spirit regardless of varying opinions.

Knowledge of God doesn't help us follow his words.

A faithful life is an adventure. It requires us to be beyond our knowledge. The Israelites said God is their protector, and he is alive. However, when they saw giant people in Canaan, they were terrified. They said they believed in God, but they actually didn't. In this case, we can say that the knowledge in our brain doesn't have power over us.

They're against God.

A knowledge-driven life leads an individual to become a rationalist. It leads them to be against the works of the Holy Spirit, God, and other people. Simply put, they're against the Holy Spirit.

> *The mind governed by the flesh is hostile to God; it does not submit to God's law, nor can it do so.*
> *Romans 8:7*

3. How can we tell when our lives are driven by a relationship with God?

Nothing can break our relationship with God.

> *For I am convinced that neither death nor life, neither angels nor demons, neither the present nor the future, nor any powers, neither height nor depth, nor anything else in all creation, will be able to separate us from the love of God that is in Christ Jesus our Lord.*
> *Romans 8:38-39*

Our behaviors or sins can't break our relationship with God like that of a parent to a child. It is the truth.

The relationship with God gives us the power to rule the world.

Noah's life was led by his relationship with God. It enabled him to continue building the ark for 120 years, regardless of others' insults, criticisms, and judgment. As for Noah, he lived a life that no one supported. He lived with loneliness and pressure, but he completed what God said to him. The ancestors of faith in Hebrews 11 did the same.

It was possible because their lives were led by their relationship with God, not their knowledge. Their inner being was having an intimate relationship with God.

4. The way to live a life led by one's relationship with God

First, we need to be honest before God and admit that we need his help so that we can better get to know him. Without his help, we wouldn't be able to achieve this goal.

Second, God sees who is desperately seeking him, so we need to exert effort in seeking his words that can speak to our inner being.

Third, we need to be honest in our relationship with him. We should not try to prove ourselves or impress him through our actions or knowledge. Showing him how faithful we are and how much we sacrificed for him doesn't build a relationship with him.

Watch out for false prophets. They come to you in sheep's clothing, but inwardly they are ferocious wolves. By their fruit you will recognize them. Do people pick grapes from thornbushes, or figs from thistles? Likewise, every good tree bears good fruit, but a bad tree bears bad fruit.
Matthew 7:15-17

5. Biblical Inner Healing is for the relationship-driven life

God wrote his first commandment to his people on a piece of stone; it was written not inside the people's hearts.

As a result, people knew the commandment as information. Now, God is writing his commandment inside our hearts through the Holy Spirit, and Biblical Inner Healing is here to facilitate this process. The only way to let your heart receive the word of God is through building a sound relationship with him.

To have God's word written inside us, our inner being must be able to listen to God's word.

It's our inner being, not the outside, which causes issues in our lives. Therefore, to see changes in our lives, our inner being must be changed, and they must hear God's words for us to achieve renewal.

Our inner being is covered by the walls we have built with the past and our grudges. These walls must be destroyed to allow us to listen to God's words.

Such a wall, which has covered our inner being, has been built not by accident but by past experiences. Therefore, we can't expect it to collapse by itself. Fortunately,

God gives us the power to destroy this wall that blocks our inner being.

The Biblical Inner Healing leads you to listen to God's words, which can give you the power to destroy the past and all the grudges that have blocked your inner being from reaching God.[32]

---

[32] See Session 10 to understand how past experiences and grudges build the wall that covers our inner being.

SESSION 3

WHO AM I?

Can you tell who you are?

If you genuinely know yourself, you can embrace yourself. You won't be ashamed of yourself. See yourself in the mirror. What does your reflection tell you? Do you see anything that needs to be fixed?

Throw out things that you shouldn't have. Begin a new life by keeping only the essentials from God.

This session aims to help you see yourself in the eyes of God, not yours.

PURPOSE OF THE SESSION

When you don't know who you are, you become vulnerable — no more than a puppet manipulated by others. You become fatalistic and waste your life, missing precious gifts from God.

Every confusion in your life starts from not knowing yourself. What does it mean when we say, "I know who I am?" If you say, "I know who I am," you can answer the following questions:

"Where are you from?"
"Where are you heading to?"
"What is your value?"

Knowing your name, job, address, or nationality doesn't mean you already know who you are. You can change your name. Your job will be gone when you retire. You can move to another address. You can even change your nationality.

If you meet children and ask who they are, they would probably say their names and hide behind their parents. Children have but their names, as they don't have jobs or licenses yet. Aside from their names, the only people who can establish who they are would be their parents.

This is what humans know about themselves. People think about their jobs, positions, or parents when defining who they are. However, when these are gone, people are lost and become confused about their identities.

Changeable titles and circumstances don't define who we are. Rather, it is the unchangeable things in us that define who we are. Therefore, we may ask, "What is it about my identity that lasts?"

No one has ever answered this question, but Jesus. He knows the exact answer to the following questions:

"Where are you from?"
"Where are you heading to?"

Compare your answers with those of Jesus. Do you see the difference? This is the first step you need to take to know who you are.

WHO AM I?

1. Where are you from?

People who made a mockery of Jesus asked him,

"Where are you from?"

They asked the question not because they wanted to know where Jesus was from. It was actually a discriminative and microaggressive statement. They asked such a question to make fun of Jesus and manifest their rejection. On that question, Jesus told them that he was from God, not by himself.

Jesus's answer

Jesus said to them, "If God were your Father, you would love me, for I have come here from God. I have not come on my own; God sent me.
John 8:42

Your answer

If people who disrespect you ask you the question, "Where are you from?" What would be your answer? How would you react?

2. Where are you heading to?

Jesus's answer

I am going back to my father.

I came from the Father and entered the world; now I am leaving the world and going back to the Father.
John 16:28

Your answer

Our lives go to the place we are heading to. However, if we don't exactly know where we are headed, our lives end up directionless, no matter how hard we try. What happens if a driver doesn't know the destination? God doesn't want us to be drivers who don't know their destinations.

3. Who are you?

Jesus's answer

I am the bread of life.

> *Then Jesus declared, "I am the bread of life. Whoever comes to me will never go hungry, and whoever believes in me will never be thirsty."*
> *John 6:35*

I am the way and the truth and the life.

> *Jesus answered, "I am the way and the truth and the life. No one comes to the Father except through me."*
> *John 14:6*

Your answer

Some would answer that they are a student, a brilliant individual, or even a loser. Whatever answer you have, it is the answer you have chosen. Therefore, it is temporary, subjective, and changeable in any circumstances. We need to hear what the creator who made us says about this.

4. What do you live for?

Jesus's answer

And this is the will of him who sent me, that I shall lose none of all those he has given me, but raise them up at the last day. For my Father's will is that everyone who looks to the Son and believes in him shall have eternal life, and I will raise them up at the last day.
John 6:39-40

The one who sent me is with me; he has not left me alone, for I always do what pleases him.
John 8:29

Jesus lived his life not for him, but for the will of God who sent him. Jesus lived as he had said. As he knew who sent him, he could continue his way of life, regardless of persecution and mockery from others.

Your answer

Some people live to win, while others live not to be disrespected. Some people live for more power, while others prefer pleasure. Some people live because they just can't die. Being a Christian doesn't mean you live your life for God. Instead, you need to look into your mind and see the motivation that leads your life.

Here's one easy way to know your motivation for life. At what moment in your life do you feel most vulnerable? Is it because of a person or a situation? Now, try to answer the following questions:

What do you think of the most?
What makes you most vulnerable?

What are your answers? These are what you live for.

Do you see the difference between Jesus's answer and yours? What's the biggest difference?

Jesus's answer didn't change over time. Regardless of the changing circumstances, Jesus had the same answer. In comparison, our answers tend to change depending on the situation.

If the answers that describe us change over time, then it should not be an answer that tells us who we are.

People say things that they believe. They think what they say is the truth. However, from Jesus' perspective, to tell the truth, we have to meet the following criteria:

First, to speak the truth, we need to know the raison d'etre.

> *Jesus answered, "Even if I testify on my own behalf, my testimony is valid, for I know where I came from and where I am going. But you have no idea where I come from or where I am going."*
> *John 8:14*

Second, to speak the truth, we need to stand by the one who sent us.

> But if I do judge, my decisions are true, because I am not alone. I stand with the Father, who sent me. In your own Law it is written that the testimony of two witnesses is true. I am one who testifies for myself; my other witness is the Father, who sent me.
> John 8:16-18

Is your answer "Yes?" If not, we need to be humbler to put down our own thoughts before Jesus.

5. How do people build their own identities?

Based on judgment by others

This is because people can't find the answer by themselves. We find the answer for ourselves through relationships with people who are deeply involved in our lives, such as family, teachers, relatives, and friends. Furthermore, media and culture also impact our answers. We create our own identity and issue our own "ID cards" based on the information we have gathered. Our identity is a creature by ourselves, and it shapes our lives. It has nothing to do with being right or wrong.

Unfortunately, we can't tell whether or not the identity we adopted for ourselves is right or wrong. Thus, more often than not, people have a wrong or "fake ID card." We make it based on our relationship with the people closest. We can't make an authentic ID card by ourselves. While it is wrong and fake, it still has substantial power over our lives.

6. The three most common ID cards that are fake and wrong

The ID card that says, "I'm a nobody"

People often hold this ID card when they haven't been accepted and have not received love from their parents. If you have been told by your parents that "You are useless" or "I don't want you in my life" for your entire life, how can you have self-esteem?

Immature parents see their children as bothersome when they are tired. They are not aware of their actions or how they can hurt their child. When children are continuously exposed to this kind of negativity, they begin to feel bad about themselves. They might also think that they were only born by accident, and when they harbor such thoughts, unintentionally, they would think that they can't be responsible for their lives. They would then adopt a fatalistic attitude toward life, thinking everything in life happens by accident.

However, it is neither valid nor true in God's eyes.

So God created mankind in his own image, in the image of God he created them; male and female he created them.
Genesis 1:27

No one was born by accident. Even though your parents may have had you unintentionally, even though no one congratulated you when you were born, you are special to God because God planned your birth.

David proclaimed that God will receive him even though his parents rejected him (Psalms 27:10).

According to the Bible, we were planned by God, even while we were in the mother's womb. He didn't make us just for fun. He has a plan and purpose for us. We were born for a reason. It was not our parents who planned and made us. Therefore, our parents can't tell us the reason why we were born.

Biological parents may decide to dump their babies or abandon and assault their children. However, God has never abandoned you. He is your real parent. It can be harder to meet your real parent—God—than your biological parents. However, you will meet him as long as you keep seeking him. Then, you will realize that he has been seeking to meet you far harder than you did.

I revealed myself to those who did not ask for me; I was found by those who did not seek me. To a nation that did not call on my name, I said, 'Here am I, here am I.'
Isaiah 65:1

It was not you who found God. He has made continuous efforts so that you will eventually notice him. Still, he is doing his best to meet you.

The ID card that says, "I am a failure. I am useless"

People often hold this ID card because the world judges people through their appearances and labels. The world has made many standards against which to compare and score individuals. Thus, people compete with one another to get a higher score. When we have a low score, we put on ourselves a label that says "failure." This label may be invisible, but it could be firmly stuck inside us.

However, this is not how God sees people. He doesn't use the standards of the world to judge us.

Interestingly, people who get high scores may still label themselves "failures." For example, Saul was brilliant. God chose him as a king. However, he was obsessed with his inferiority, and so he wasted his whole life feeling inferior to David.

Feeling inferior or seeing oneself as a failure is not just for people with "low scores." It is actually more like a personal issue and is an outcome of spiritual deception.

If we don't know that we are fooled, we are likely to spend our lives aiming for a higher score. If we can't get a higher score, we would consider ourselves a failure, feel insecure, and then blame God for it.

For example, there was a young man who felt inferior

because of his short height such that he only focused on it. It was his only prayer. "God, please make me taller," he would pray.

He thought God had made him short to put him through a troubled life. He blamed God and his parents. He asked his parents to pay for a surgery that would make him taller. They were poor, but he asked them to pay for it anyway, even declaring, "I will not see anyone before I have the surgery."

He was stubborn. He was obsessed with an issue that couldn't be fixed. He was wasting his youth doing nothing.

Meanwhile, there's another story of one Genzo Mizuno, who became a quadriplegic after an illness when he was in fourth grade. He wasn't able to do anything but blink his eyes. He couldn't even sit by himself. One day, he became a Christian and found out how God saw him. His hopeless life was eventually filled with his worship of God. He showed his heart to God through his poetry. This is how his life has inspired and touched other's lives.

His poetry is full of worship and gratitude to God. There's no single word that shows his pain due to his body. How can a man lead this kind of life?

He saw himself through the eyes of God, not the world. He knew who he was in the eyes of God, and for him, this was the truth. As he held the real ID card issued by God, he was not fooled by deceptions. The harsh words of people were powerless before him.

Have you ever wondered what God's priority was when

he made you? It was not your appearance. It was your inside, your inner being, which is far more fundamental and lasts forever. If you blame God for your appearance, you can't continue to have a good relationship with him.

> *Do not conform to the pattern of this world, but be transformed by the renewing of your mind. Then you will be able to test and approve what God's will is—his good, pleasing and perfect will.*
> Romans 12:2

Putting appearance as a priority in our hearts is what the rest of the world does. It is how a demon sees. We should not be fooled.

The ID card that says, "I am better than anyone"

People often hold this ID card because they compare themselves with others and are arrogant. Often, people become arrogant through their childhood experiences. Their parents and relatives may have always told them that they were more brilliant than others, making them believe that they are indeed better than others. Thus, they become obsessed with receiving that compliment. When there's someone better than them, they feel hostile against that person. They can't accept anyone better than them. They compete to be at the top of everything. They only feel secure when they receive a compliment. These people can't take a rest or have peace in their minds. They also cannot have sympathy, nor can they truly love anyone.

The world that has the demon as a king is full of competition and comparison. However, in the world of God, no one is inferior or superior. Everyone has their own talents. God's world is to serve, and God tells us to serve others if we want to win.

"Am I valuable?"

The answer to this question can be found in the Bible:

"You were created in the image of God who can have a relationship with him." (Genesis 1:27)
"You are so loved that God gave his one and only Son for you to have eternal life." (John 3:16)

These are the answers that last forever. They don't change under any circumstances. This is how valued you are in the eyes of God. The ID card issued by God is the one that we should hold, as no one can change it or fake it. Therefore, to achieve maturity and renewal from our past experiences, the first thing to do is find our real ID card issued by God. This ID card doesn't have a validity date. When we are sick, when we get fired from our jobs, when we are nobody in the world, this ID will still be valid because it is issued by God. We have to cherish this ID card and hold it deep inside us.

CASE

Knowing who I am in God gave me freedom

I am a high school teacher. I am also a senior member of my church. I came to the BIH seminar with my wife. I didn't think I had an unsolved issue or pain to resolve. So I didn't expect a lot. I just let God do whatever he wants to do.

Before I attended the BIH seminar, I understood inner healing as a psychological session. However, I soon found out that I was wrong. It has nothing to do with psychology. It was so real, like I was having surgery.

I teach literature at school, but I am not sure how to describe what I have been through. In short, I experienced the Holy Spirit working in me during the seminar. It happened during the session. Dr. Kim said that we need to make the central foundation inside us to have Jesus Christ. I wanted it too. So I prayed in a whispering voice:

"I want to have the foundation in the center of my heart for you, Lord."

Suddenly, I felt a sense of peace and joy inside me. I knew it was the Holy Spirit. It was like a flow of pure water in me. I read the Bible saying something like the flow of pure water in our hearts. I thought it was just a metaphor, but I really felt that inside me!

The next session was about forgiveness. Dr. Kim told us to tell God what happened and forgive by letting God take care of it. Following the instructions of Dr. Kim, I tried to remember things from my childhood. I thought about my mother. She gave birth to me when she was 22 years old. I prayed and wanted God to do something for my mother, and I saw this scene in my mind. There was something dark—a black object. It was like a moving creature, but it was so vague that I wasn't sure what it was. I wanted to know what it was, and this clear vision came up. There was Jesus. He was standing on some greenery. There were evergreen trees behind him. He was standing against the sunlight, and he told me:

"Honey, I also didn't have a father who completely gets me."

With a calming and comforting tone, he continued:

"But I am your father. Aren't I?"

It was at that moment that the black thing I saw in me disappeared. I felt like it had left a clean hole in me without any pain. I felt pure. I was in tears and overwhelmed with freshness, joy, peace, and calmness. I haven't experienced anything like this. I kept saying, 'What the...what the...'

I felt like Jesus wanted me to open up the Bible. So I picked up my Bible and somehow read John 14:16–18. There was a sentence that spoke to me:

"I will ask the Father to give you another advocate to be with you forever. I will not leave you as orphans."

I vividly felt the wind blow through my heart. I couldn't help but take off my jacket and literally asked my friend whether my heart was okay.

I didn't know I had sorrow in me. I lost my father when I was only five months old. I was the only son in my family and among all my relatives. I had all that pressure from being the only son in the family and being a child without a father. I always worked so hard so that people can't call me a child without a father. I wanted to be powerful. It has been an enormous pressure in my life. The black thing that I saw in the scene was my burned heart from all the pressure and pain that I endured.

Now, I understand why I had all that troubles with my mother and a deepening sense of guilt. I realized, 'My life never has had a rest. I was in a never-ending race. I tried so hard that others couldn't notice that I had no father.'

I felt that God allowed me to rest. It was the first time. I felt relieved. I thought to myself, 'My real father is God. He gets me better than anyone else. He gets me better than I do. He is my father!'

I was a Christian, but it was all new to me.

I came home. I sat with my wife and children, who all went to the seminar with me. We prayed together. It was like heaven. My children kept telling me we needed to have a party, as I found my father.

I now have a father who gets me. I don't even need to tell him when I am sad. He knows everything!

A few days later, while I was praying, I couldn't say anything. I was wailing like a little child looking for his father. I wailed for hours. I didn't have this kind of relationship with God before. All I did was say the things that I wanted.

I didn't even wonder where God was, and I didn't have any problems with it. Now, I feel him as my father. I can cry in front of him, and I can rest with him.

My wife has witnessed these tremendous changes in my life, and she told me,

"You were like a bomb about to explode. Now, I see the detonator has been removed from you."

SESSION 4

WHAT DOES THE BIBLE SAY ABOUT HUMAN BEINGS?

What is Jesus's promise from the Cross? What does the Bible tell us about humans?

Philosophical theories may impress you, yet they can't heal you. Keep Jesus's words from the Cross for your inner healing.

PURPOSE OF THE SESSION

To be healed, our minds and our hearts must be diagnosed first. To avoid misdiagnosis, there should be no errors in understanding how our minds and hearts work. Who knows the most about how our minds and hearts work? It is God, and he assures us of this truth through the Bible.

The only way to avoid misdiagnosis is to understand our minds and hearts based on the Bible. Therefore, the aim of this session is to help you better understand the minds and hearts of humans, based on the perspective offered by the Bible.

People who study humans

First, who possesses an exact and accurate understanding of humans? Modern studies on humans have unique features. While they raise serious questions about humans, they have yet to question the ultimate reality or ontology.[33]

Today, many are interested in discussing the question, "What is a human?" However, the discussions are unable to determine the right answer, as they miss a fundamental, accompanying question: "Where does a human come from?"

Trying to know humans without knowing God, the creator of humans, leads to the wrong answer. It creates the wrong perspective on humans, and, of course, it brings consequences.

To date, various perspectives have been proposed to understand humans, and we choose one of them. Within the concept of Biblical Inner Healing, taking the Bible's perspective in understanding humans is the first step toward inner healing.

---

[33] Hoekma, Anthony (1994) *Created in God's Image*. Wm. B. Eerdmans Publishing Co.

WHAT DOES THE BIBLE SAY ABOUT HUMAN BEINGS?

1. What is a "decent man?"

In the world in which we live, things that give power to people, such as status, reputation, fame, knowledge, and wealth, define who can be considered a decent human being.

However, the Bible has different criteria. God has his plumb line to determine whether we are decent in his eyes, and thus far, the only person who has ever satisfied his criteria is Jesus Christ.

2. According to God's plumb line, there has been only one decent person thus far

What is the role of the spirit in a human being?

Among all his creatures, God only allowed human beings to have a spirit. This gives us a unique and extraordinary power that allows us to have a relationship with God. It is placed at the core of our being.

Our spirit is endless, and because of it, we can love God and have a relationship with him. Our spirit also lets us have wisdom in our minds and know God. Indeed, we can't know God without having a spirit. This process can only be made possible through our spirit.

What is the role of the body?

The body is the part of a human being that God created through soil. It can rule and touch all creatures God has made.[34]

Humans also have a natural instinct that serves to protect our bodies. It lets us know what we need to do to keep us safe.

When the body is dehydrated, it makes us feel thirsty, so we are prompted to drink water. Similarly, we can't

---

[34] God blessed them and said to them, "Be fruitful and increase in number, fill the earth and subdue it. Rule over the fish in the sea and the birds in the sky and over every living creature that moves on the ground."

keep our bodies safe if we don't have this instinct. Having instinct is not inferior or sinful. No one thinks a car is guilty because it hits a person. Likewise, the body and instinct are instruments that follow the order of a human mind.

When the Holy Spirit communes with our spirits, it makes our minds healthy. A healthy mind makes our bodies healthy, and our bodies become the instrument and church of God.

What is the mind?

There are two completely different dimensions inside us: the spiritual dimension and the physical dimension. The mind is like a bridge or tunnel that connects these two completely different dimensions.

Our mind reveals our spirit through our body. A healthy mind reveals a healthy spirit, while a sinful mind reveals a wicked spirit—a demon. When individuals allow demons to take over their minds, their bodies become tools to harm the world. Thus, whether a person is a scientist or a schoolteacher, as long as they let evil govern their minds, then they can cause harm and destruction to others around them.

Moreover, when individuals allow a demon to govern their spirit, they become destructive puppets for the demon. The Bible strictly bans us from being near such evil spirits.[35]

Figure 4[36]

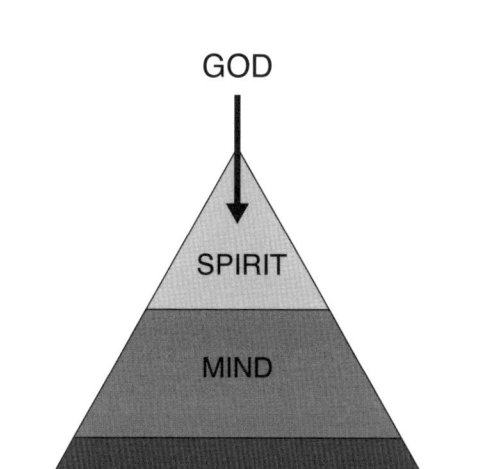

God is everywhere, and we are in his presence. Thus, because God is a spirit, we can have a relationship with God through our spirit. Having a relationship with God gives our spirit the wisdom and power to rule over our minds, which in turn, rule over our bodies.

3. The failure of human beings and its impact

It changes the spirit.

---

[35] Let no one be found among you who sacrifices their son or daughter in the fire, who practices divination or sorcery, interprets omens, engages in witchcraft. (Deuteronomy 18:9-14)

[36] Marshall, Tom (2000) *Free Indeed.* Sovereign World.

When a man broke a promise he had made with God, the Spirit of God immediately left his spirit. (Genesis 6:3). Since then, the spirit of a man has lost its power and role, signifying its death.

Except for human beings, all creatures disappear when they die. However, as we have a spirit that is not created by soil, we cannot fully "disappear."[37]

If people cannot be reunited with God during their lifetimes, they may experience an everlasting disconnection from God. This is what Jesus told us to be afraid of: the so-called "second death."

It changes the mind and body.

When the core of a human being—the spirit—loses its power, the mind will still work, along with "feelings" and the "human will." However, there's no vision nor direction. Thus, a person becomes confused like a soldier without his or her general. The person can continue to think, but be unable to reach the truth. Deception fools a person, and as this happens, the person will become powerless to make the right choices, leading him or her to ask the following questions:

"Who am I?"

"Who is this asking the question?"

"Am I worthy enough?"

---

[37] And the dust returns to the ground it came from, and the spirit returns to God who gave it.(Ecclesiastes 12:7)

"What am I doing?"

People who abandoned their origins face the same consequences. They might perceive that God abandoned them, even if it was them who actually abandoned God first. They feel rejected and humiliated. Nothing in the world can comfort their minds. They ask a question, but they won't hear any answers. They feel that they have lost something huge in their lives, but they don't know what it is. They feel isolated, with an overwhelming sense of loss.

People who carry the sense of loss and feel abandoned can't avoid its impact on their bodies. It's like a virus that causes disease and illness. The demon continues to tell lies and deceptions to people to bring them to the valley of the shadow of death.[38]

One lady who shared her story suffered from anxiety and depression due to her marriage.

During the BIH seminar, I saw this vision when I was a newborn baby. My father threw me away because I was not a boy. My parents remarried each other. Since birth, my father has hated and abandoned me because I was a girl. He didn't want me to go to school.

"I won't even blink my eye if you die," he always told me.

When I was in elementary school, I worked at a farm. Sometimes, he locked the door when I came late from

---

[38] John 10:10

hanging out with my friends. My mother would bring me dinner outside without him knowing, but sometimes, when my mother didn't bring me dinner, I had nothing to eat and stayed outside—alone.

A few years later, my brother was born. Whenever I wanted to eat something, I had to ask my brother. My parents gave everything to him, and I could have leftovers. I never thought it was unfair.

One day, I didn't understand why, but I wanted my life to be over. I felt devastated that no one would care. I was scared and in pain, so I cried and screamed in my room. 'Why was I born? I shouldn't be born. Where am I going if I die? My family won't care.' Since then, this pain would surface from time to time, but I have no idea what to do.

Is she destined to feel hopeless in her life? Is there no way to get out of the pain?

If there was no way to escape, people wouldn't feel bad or be in pain, even though they are in the valley of the shadow of death. People feel pain because they know there's something better; that this isn't what they should feel. It also means that they know the light exists in this world that we live in. Anyone can find the light and get free.

Some people reject and blame God. They say it is God's fault for giving free will to humans, allowing them to make bad choices that result in terrible outcomes. They say it is God's fault, and now he even punishes people.

Of course, God knew humans would eventually fail to obey his words. However, he also had a plan to fix things. He planned to send his only son, Jesus, to take all the punishments humans should have. Jesus died on the Cross even before Genesis.[39]

God created us in his plan with great love. Here, we can find an answer that can help us resolve the pain we may be experiencing. God told Adam and Eve the answer to life and gave them an opportunity to make the right choice. He told them the answer before they made a choice. Today, he gives us, once again, the opportunity to make the right choice. This time, as with Adam and Eve, he had already shown us the answer to life with his great love through the Cross. Now we know the answer, and this is our final opportunity to make the right choice.

4. The Cross of Jesus Christ and its impact on our lives

The Cross of Jesus Christ has the power to renew a person who believes in it. A person has three components that may be renewed: body, mind, and spirit. Each area has different procedures and timelines.

Spirit: Being reborn, being anointed by the Holy Spirit and his presence

---

[39] Sauer, Eric (1994). *From Eternity to Eternity*. Paternoster Press.

Being reborn occurs immediately when a person receives Jesus as the Lord. It lasts forever. No one deserves it, but it is a gift freely given by God.[40] Furthermore, God allows each person who receives Jesus to receive the Holy Spirit in one's inner being as well.[41]

The Holy Spirit empowers a person and helps those who became a child of God develop into someone who is like God's son.[42]

Mind: Healing, new architecture

The human mind doesn't experience immediate renewal when it receives Jesus. When we receive Jesus, we enter into the beginning to renew our minds. It is not the same as editing or revising. The Holy Spirit works in us to build an entirely new mind, just like building a new architecture. We can be like a child of God and imbibe Jesus's personality.[43] When it happens, the mind can listen to God's words and exercise the will to follow him. Feelings and emotions are renewed. Indeed, there's no broken and corrupted mind that the Holy Spirit can't renew.

---

[40] Very truly I tell you, whoever hears my word and believes him who sent me has eternal life and will not be judged but has crossed over from death to life (John 5:24); And this is the testimony: God has given us eternal life, and this life is in his son. Whoever has the son has life; whoever does not have the Son of God does not have life. I write these things to you who believe in the name of the Son of God so that you may know that you have eternal life.(1 John 5:11–13)

[41] John 14:16-17

[42] Session 6 explains how the Holy Spirit empowers a person.

[43] See Galatians 5:22; Ephesians 4:15. It tells the fruit of the Spirit.

Body: Becoming holy to glorify God

What's the impact of the Cross of Jesus Christ on the human body?

On the one hand, when the human spirit and mind become old and weak, the human body also becomes weak and a tool for sin. On the other hand, when the spirit becomes renewed and healthy, it impacts the body. Jesus heals and sets our body free from the bondages of the past. The impact of Jesus Christ is on everyone and everything.

However, to reveal such a blessing, we must cooperate with the Holy Spirit in us. Our inner selves have to follow God's words. If we refuse to work with the Holy Spirit, there won't be any renewal.

Even though a person sees a miracle and has a spiritual experience, it doesn't necessarily change one's mind and perspective. The spiritual experience can allow a person to have a spiritual gift and say extraordinary things in the short term. However, without renewal in one's mind, a person with such a gift can hurt others and harm the Christian community.

We all need renewal and new architecture in our minds. Unfortunately, not all of us feel the need to be healed.

5. Neglecting the need to be healed leads a person to be an immature Christian, controlled by the flesh

There was a couple known in their community as lovebirds. They were considered an ideal couple and even led the family ministry in their church. However, their real lives were not happy at all. The husband physically abused his wife and children. At the same time, he was afraid of people knowing what was really happening in his family. So did the wife and children. They all didn't want others to know that their home permitted domestic violence. After each act of violence, the husband blamed himself and told the wife that he loved her. He wanted to stop, but failed to do so every time. It was so bad that the wife even attempted suicide. This was how they lived for twenty years.

When we face issues in our minds, we tend to think:

"I'm born with this. I can't fix this."

"This is my natural personality."

"I am not the only one who lives with weakness. Everyone does."

"We are all sinners. I can't help."

"No one can fix this."

"I should pray more to fix this."

However, this is not the right way to go. The renewal of minds only happens to people who truly become God's children. God told us to have a new mind, and for this, we have a plumb line: Jesus. We should renew our minds with this divine plumb line.

6. The church community can provide great support to help renew our minds

There was a Christian lady who was having a troubled relationship with her mother-in-law. Her in-laws went to the same church as her and held senior positions at the church. Thus, she found it difficult to share her issues with anyone from the church.

Over the years, she suffered from insomnia and depression. Her psychiatrist told her to do something new to release her stress. One suggested driving a car.

One day, she was driving with her parents and family and got into a car accident. One of her family members was killed. She felt scared and guilty. She thought she was being punished because she hated her mother-in-law. As a result, she stopped going to church altogether. Her body became weaker and weaker from mental illness.

"I wish I could talk to anyone from the church. They are my good friends, with whom I have spent several years of my life. But I can't tell them about the pains in my heart... and the issues I have with in-laws. I was afraid of being judged."

A church is a community for healing. One person doesn't have much power. However, when people gather together as part of Jesus's body, there is power that can help others. God uses people to help and comfort people.

In building new architecture in our minds, the encouragement and support given by the Christian community can play a significant role.

However, when a church strictly emphasizes rules over the Gospel, it is difficult for members of the community to share their minds with others. A church where people find it difficult to show their weakness can't be a place for healing. If we trust our fellow Christians not to judge others, then we can share our weaknesses. We can pray for one another and experience divine healing.

If people don't feel secure sharing their issues in their church community, they may try to find wisdom outside of the church. They expect wisdom from humanism—not from the Bible—to heal their minds.

A middle-aged man called me one time and shared his story. He was an ordinary office worker. He was known to be a faithful man in his church. Many people had asked him to go to theological college. He wanted to take it seriously and wanted to know what God thought of this. So he went to a prayer house with his friend. There, they met the director of the prayer house who joined them in prayer. While praying, the director poked his friend's eye with his finger as some kind of spiritual behavior. He felt uncomfortable and thought something was off. However, he decided to stay until the prayer ended.

Since then, he has become insecure and even suffered from insomnia. He had taken pills for over two years, but his condition didn't get better. It had already impacted his work. He discussed it with the pastor, who suggested meeting a psychiatrist. He felt devastated when he heard this, because he was already taking pills but didn't see any progress. He felt abandoned by God. He was afraid of losing his family and work.

Some ministers would say, "The church is a place to give spiritual help. It is a place to talk about heaven and Jesus. If you have issues in your mind, see a psychiatrist." They reject the idea that the Holy Spirit can heal mental issues. However, they are incorrect in this respect.

In fact, there's nothing wrong with seeing a psychiatrist. What's wrong is these ministers' dichotomous idea of separating spiritual issues from mental issues. As we already know, the spirit, mind, and body of humans cannot be separated, and Jesus works on all of these to help humans achieve renewal.

God can heal any weakness in people and their bodies. If more than 80 percent of illness in the human body is due to mental issues, then isn't it natural for Jesus to want to heal our mental issues as well?

When a church refuses to see the work of the Holy Spirit in healing people, it becomes just a theater where people act and perform. Some say there are not many churches in revival in high-GDP countries, such as Western Europe and North America. However, this is not correct in all cases. Some churches in the region continue to experience growth and revival. These churches all seek the work of the Holy Spirit to heal the body, mind, and spirit with healthy fellowships.

Human minds are like a deep sea that cannot be seen

easily. However, God sees our mind crystal clear as he created it. He knows the causes that lead us to sorrow, loneliness, emptiness, and anger.

For a church to be a place to comfort and heal people, the following efforts can help.

A church needs to put more effort than a psychologist or psychiatrist into understanding the psychological issues of its fellow members. Although Job's friends were not good advisors, they waited seven days with Job before giving him advice. If a church puts an effort into listening and expressing sympathy with its fellow members, such as Job's friend, who waited for seven days, a church will be more empowered.

Sometimes, psychological approaches and information can help extend our understanding of how minds work. But what's more important is the explanation from the Bible. We have to stick to words from the Bible to understand our minds. If we believe and try, we will find an answer from the Bible. We know God and others only as much as we know ourselves. We can help others only as much as we understand.

7. The mind should be renewed

Renewing includes two aspects: demolishing the old parts and building new ones. The Holy Spirit welcomes and leads the procedure.

The Holy Spirit reveals and demolishes the parts that have gone wrong.

No matter how old or strong it is, the Holy Spirit gently destroys it and reveals the fake shelter that we have created to hide our weaknesses.

For Israelites, strictly following religious rule was their fake shelter. They kept the sabbath, gave tithes, and fasted. So they believed God loved them. However, God revealed how it was wrong for them to worship idols at the sanctuary (Ezekiel 8:9–10). The spiritual leaders of the Israelites worshiped idols at the sanctuary made for God. When people go to church, but their hearts are not with God, this shows the duplicity of humans who worship the things they wish to pursue.

An idol is what we care about the most. Meanwhile, inner healing is a procedure that needs to be done before destroying the idols hidden inside us. Inner healing reveals the remaining sins in us that have been hidden.

Figure 5

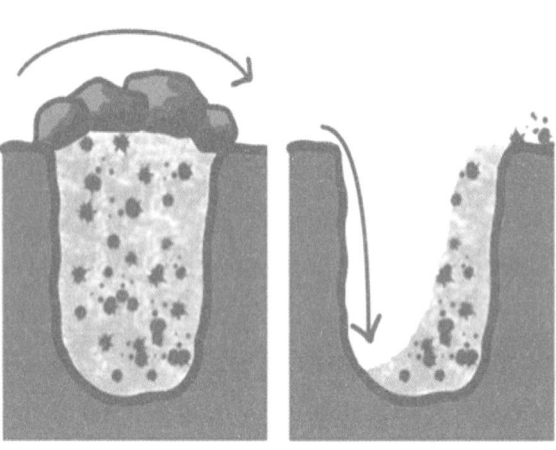

In the figure, the hole refers to the wounded part inside us, filled with sorrow and pain. The hole is like a trashcan filled with everything we want to hide. We put heavy rocks to cover the hole and hide what's inside, so that it would seem like everything is normal. However, the Holy Spirit wants us to remove the rocks and see through what has happened, as the things we put inside the hole impact our lives today. The Holy Spirit wants us to know that we have him, and we are not alone. The Holy Spirit wants us to start to go through things inside the hole, take everything out, and clean it with him. He wants us to be free from the hole, its hostile powers, and all the negativities from the past.

The process of healing is to worship God with all of our hearts (John 4:24). The Israelites denied that they had idols; they also denied the sins inside them. When we deny the presence of sins inside us, there's no healing. Without healing, pain and sorrow will remain with us for the rest of our lives (Jeremiah 30:12–15).

The Holy Spirit reveals false shelter and idols in us because they are the bondage that keeps our inner being sick. When the bondage is revealed and broken, our inner beings can mature in God. It is also important to mention that the healing and building of new architecture by the Holy Spirit in us is not just to comfort us (Ezekiel 13:10–14). The renewal of our inner being is something that has to happen. Sometimes, it may lead to actual pain, much like having surgery. This is what happens when, for example, a humiliating event from the past comes up.

The Holy Spirit is glad to build a new building in us, and only a building built on God's plumb line is solid. When we confess our sins before the Cross and pursue life from God's perspective, we help the Holy Spirit work its way through us.

The Holy Spirit builds a solid, new mind.

1) The Holy Spirit lays a cornerstone

> *So this is what the Sovereign Lord says: "See, I lay a stone in Zion, a tested stone, a precious cornerstone for a sure foundation; the one who relies on it will never be stricken with panic."*
> *Isaiah 28:16*

God came to us to be the cornerstone of our lives.

What we need to do after receiving Jesus is replace the old cornerstone with a new one. Christians often neglect to change their old ways of life and thinking. However, believing in God doesn't mean that our old way of life is automatically renewed. We need to replace it with the help of the Holy Spirit.

2) The Holy Spirit gives us the wisdom to understand God and ourselves

> *I will give them a heart to know me, that I am the Lord. They will be my people, and I will be their God, for they will return to me with all their heart.*
> *Jeremiah 24:7*

> *The wisdom of the prudent is to give thought to their ways, but the folly of fools is deception.*
> *Proverbs 14:8*

The wisdom from God matures our inner being. The wisdom that comes from God is a gift. Indeed, God said that anyone with a clean heart will see God.

3) We can have intimacy with God. This is what Jesus wants us to have the most

That all of them may be one, Father, just as you are in me and I am in you. May they also be in us so that the world may believe that you have sent me.
John 17:21

SESSION 5

BITTER ROOT AND FORGIVENESS

What does forgiveness mean?

Why do we have to forgive?

How did others forgive?

PURPOSE OF THE SESSION

Being disrespected or betrayed leaves traumatic damage. The experience of being hurt by others becomes a channel through which demons can destroy our lives. It harms our personalities, relationships, and lives. The only way to be free from bitterness is forgiveness, which is a fundamental step to helping heal our wounds.

This session is intended to help us have actual forgiveness.

BITTER ROOT AND FORGIVENESS

1. Symptoms of an unforgiving person

- You try not to show interest in someone.
- You expect attention and take it for granted.
- You overly praise or criticize someone.
- You tend to be obsessed with your friends.
- You are happy outside but frustrated inside.
- You are overly cautious about meeting people.
- You vividly remember when someone hurts your feelings.
- When something happens, you are overwhelmingly angry or sad.
- You spend energy criticizing someone or some group.

2. Why do we have to forgive?

- If we are unforgiving, we can feel God's forgiveness.
- If we are unforgiving and depressed, our minds are filled with harmful and hurtful memories, not God. This impacts our minds and promotes the presence of grudges and bitterness.
- If we are unforgiving, our minds will be filled with grudges. We can't get over thinking about a person we hate. It makes us resemble that person. When it happens, it makes us hate ourselves.
- If we are unforgiving, we can't break another chain of sins.
- If we are unforgiving, our spirit is weakened, which prevents us from having an intimate relationship with God.
- God's gift can't grow in you if you are holding grudges and bitterness.
- You can't receive the fruits of the Holy Spirit, and you can't have a whole, rich life that God gave to you.

Words in Galatians 5:23 describe the personality given by the Holy Spirit. If you are unforgiving, you can still preach at a church, but the fruit of the Holy Spirit in you would be limited.

3. What does God say about forgiveness?

Forgiveness is not about being neglected about someone's fault. Analyzing and making excuses for someone's fault is not forgiveness. Blaming myself for someone's fault is not forgiveness.

Some people think it is a generous move to overlook someone's fault or blame one's self. However, it is not forgiveness. As this pattern continues, disappointment and bitterness continue to grow inside. It leads to a closed mind toward others. Unless we follow forgiveness based on the Bible, none of those generous moves can't set us free from bitterness.

4. How does forgiveness work?

We can take the following steps to help nurture forgiveness inside of us:
   i. Clarify the harms and faults of an offender, which can be your family member or close friend. Still, you have to clarify the harms they gave you.
   ii. Clarify the damage in your heart.
   iii. Respect your rage and resentment. When we become overwhelmingly furious and in pain, we tend to hide and bury these feelings. We do this to protect ourselves from the anger and pain that we can't handle. However, even though we forget, anger stays with us. It pops up at some point, making us

direct our anger toward someone who is not even responsible for it. Sometimes, that someone can be ourselves, especially when it manifests as self-loathing and depression. Therefore, we need to clarify our past issues and take care of them properly.

iv. Think of God's love from the Cross and his forgiveness. Then, choose to forgive and speak it out.

v. When you speak out to God that you chose to forgive, let God be the judge.

vi. Confess that you were unforgiving. Trust God's words, and be thankful.

5. God's role and my role in forgiveness

God's role

1) My feelings

We can fake our feelings. Forgiveness is not about how we feel. If we focus on changing our feelings, we fail to truly forgive. We can't change our feelings. If we focus on things that we can't change, there will be no outcome but confusion. Thus, we must choose to forgive. Forgiveness is obedience. When we make a choice to obey God, the Holy Spirit helps us get ready for change.

2) Offender

Forgiveness may not bring changes to the offender, which can hurt us again. However, we need to remember that the offender's feelings and behaviors are beyond our authority. Rather, it is up to God.[44]

My role

The only role we have is to choose to forgive and speak it out. God ordered us to forgive. Thus, we have only two choices: to obey or not to obey God. We have to make a choice to let God be a judge so that he can take care of all the rest.

6. Why is it difficult to forgive?

- It is hard to forgive when we are jealous of an offender.
- We tend to find others' sins as bigger than ours when we have the same one. It is the habit of condemnation. It is hard to forgive when we have the same sin as an offender.
- We don't precisely know the impact of being unforgiving on our lives and spirits.
- It is hard to forgive others when we don't confess

---

[44] In the Lord's hand the king's heart is a stream of water that he channels toward all who please him.

our sins before God.
- It is hard to forgive family members or people close to us. We are afraid of them being around us and hurting us again if we forgive them.

Cunningham talked about the fear that hinders forgiveness:

"We have a fear of being hurt again if we forgive. However, forgiveness is the most important key to protecting you from further damages. Also, forgiveness gives you the healing that makes you strong enough to endure when someone hurts you again in the future." [45]

Forgiveness is not an easy path to go. However, you can't have healing in God if you don't pursue this path. God knows how weak we are. He can help us once we decide to forgive.

7. Three ways of forgiveness

Ask God to forgive your sin.

If we confess our sins, he is faithful and just and will forgive us our sins and purify us from all unrighteousness.
1 John 1:9

God has already forgiven us, even if we have not yet

---

[45] Cunningham, Loren(1989) *Winning God's Way*. Frontline Communications.

confessed our sins (Romans 5:8). Jesus sacrificed himself to forgive all our sins. However, if we don't confess sincerely before God, we can't have his forgiveness. Do not ask God, "What did I do? Was it sin?" Be honest before God and confess your sins. This is the only way to renew ourselves.

When we receive Jesus Christ, God forgives all our sins. However, we have to confess before God so that we can receive the power of forgiveness in ourselves. Even mature Christians who have a relationship with God can commit sins. When it happens, guilt captures us. However, we should focus on confessing our sins and asking for God's forgiveness.

Blaming others can never purify us from sin. We are free from sin only when we admit that we chose to sin and confess before the Cross.

Accept who you are and forgive yourself.

Failing to forgive yourself is not being modest. Rather, it only shows that you are an arrogant non-believer. As God accepts and loves you, you have to love and accept yourself as well. Being unforgiving and humiliating yourself is a rebellion against God. God doesn't want us to be prison officers who watch ourselves. Moreover, this is not the life of a Christian that God wants for us. Self-abuse happens when our focus is on ourselves. Being humble and confessing before God, on the one hand, and abusing ourselves, on the other hand, are not the same. The former lets us have a loving spirit to forgive ourselves and others, while the latter only leads to self-loathing and humiliation. The former way of life leads us to become a person who knows and spreads the power of the Cross.

Forgive people who hurt you.

This is not like forgiving every person we meet. Forgiveness also requires power, and each of us has a different level of power to forgive. Ironically, people with the strong power to forgive barely get hurt and have not many people to forgive. On the other hand, people with a weak power to forgive have so many people to forgive. Can you imagine how tiring it would be to lead a life filled with people you may need to forgive?

The point is that we need to develop our power to forgive. Each of us can do so, and the first step is to take care of the anger deep inside us.

Pray and ask God if there's any anger you are harboring from your childhood. Ask him to let you know if there's any of it deep inside you. When God helps us find the anger that has grown inside us, we complete the first step we need to take to develop our power to forgive.

8. Why do we need to forgive someone who has not apologized?

We feel uncomfortable when there's a small piece of glass on our fingers, regardless of its size. Likewise, grudges and bitterness inside us make us feel tired and anxious, regardless of their size. It robs our energy; this is what a demon wants. In contrast, God gives us peace. God wants us to be free from negative emotions and memories that hold our minds hostage. So he asks us to forgive. It is God's suggestion so that we can be better off.

God is fair. He provides the fairest and most impartial resolution because he knows everything. The fault of a person who hurts us doesn't go away because we forgive. It is the business between God and that person. While we may be victims who get hurt, we also tend to hurt God if we don't forgive. We are all sinners, forgiven even if we have not yet confessed our sins. We all hurt Jesus, but he already forgave everything before we can even ask for forgiveness.

But God demonstrates his love for us in this:
While we were still sinners, Christ died for us.
Romans 5:8

We forgive someone before they apologize, because God forgave us before we asked. It is how we can hand over to God someone who hurts us. When we forgive a person who hurts us, our role is done. We become free.

Now, it is God and that person's business.

9. Forgiveness, you can start now

Forgiving is not about allowing the wrongdoing of a person we forgive.

Forgiveness is about stepping down as a judge. It is about admitting that God is the one who has the right to judge and rule over us. It is just like laying down all the work of a judge.

Often, forgiveness doesn't remove all the resentments.

Even though resentments remain, forgiveness starts as soon as we decide to forgive. Forgiveness is much like opening the lid of a trash bin in our minds, filled with hostility and anger, and taking the time to empty it out until the day we can see it cleaned out.

Pray and ask the Holy Spirit to tell us whom we should forgive.

We think we know who to forgive. Sometimes, however, we need to forgive someone we don't expect. Past events that we can't even remember can cause us to harbor grudges inside us. Ask the Holy Spirit to let you know who to forgive and what events imprison you in such a state.

List down the names that came up. Write down what to forgive in detail.

As we learned in the previous session, a wound in us wasn't just created by itself. It was from a specific event. Think carefully about a specific event that caused a wound in you. Vagueness is not a helpful attitude to have when forgiving. Thus, try to be more specific. Instead of saying, "I forgive the person who hurt me," try to say specific words, things, behaviors, or incidents and the name of the person you are trying to forgive.

If you forgive the event that happened when you were a child, try to be that child again. Because you have grown up, you may now think, "It's not that big of a deal" when you try to forgive. However, this is not a good way to forgive. Rather, you must try to go back to the moment when you were a child. Forgive with the child's mind, not with the mind of a grown-up. Even though it may seem trivial now, it was a big deal if it hurt you.

Remember these two things.

First, God told us to forgive (Matthew 5:43–47). Second, God told us that he will hear us if we ask him anything according to his will (1 John 5:14-15). Hold the promise of God and speak out to forgive others in God.

CASE

What? I am not your mom

I am a missionary and am proud of myself as a good Christian. However, sometimes, I felt a sense of overwhelming bitterness and loneliness that made me feel bad about myself. I was often tempted to sin when it happened and looked for pleasure to ease my pain. Now, I see there was a pattern, but I didn't know.

I came to the BIH seminar and wanted to know what caused the feelings of bitterness and anger in me. While I was praying, I recalled one memory I had when I was six years old.

My parents divorced when I was three. Then, I lived with my grandmother and uncle. My father was drunk all the time, and he abused me physically and verbally. When I was six, my father remarried. At that time, because I was too young, I thought of my stepmother as my birth mother. One day, she was in the front yard, and I ran to her, calling her "Mom!" but she had this icy look on her face and told me:

"What? I am not your mom."

"......."

I could vividly feel the same feeling I had at that time. Inside my heart, there was six-year-old me. She was in tears and was so sad. I didn't think it was a big deal. I didn't know that I was hurt when she told me that, but now, I see that it hurt me. My father didn't know anything about this, even when he passed away. He told my grandmother never to allow me to live with my birth mother.

I had lived with my grandmother all my life, and it was only a few years ago when I met my birth mother. I missed her so much. However, she wasn't anything like a mother I had dreamed about. She wasn't warm or friendly to me. She often got mad at me. She told me everything was my father's fault, but I didn't want to hear her blaming my father.

My birth mother remarried and is now living with her new husband. I tried to love her. But whenever she blamed my father and hated me for being on his side, I also got mad at her. I realized that I hated my mother more than my stepmother, who abandoned me.

My father was an alcoholic, but he loved me. Then he died. I couldn't understand why my mother kept blaming her dead husband. I missed her for so long, but she disappointed me; she didn't even care. I couldn't forgive her.

When I was struggling to forgive her, God told me to

forgive her. But I couldn't. There was a cold, fixed grudge stuck inside me, filled with anger toward her.

But God helped me. I realized that I had sinned, making God sad. Yet, God melted that grudge. He let me feel his love. He let me know that I wasn't the only one who got hurt. I prayed for them.

I met God as my true mother. Because I met my true mother, I could forgive people who hurt me, including my birth mother.

CASE

How I was healed from my persistent stomach pain

My pastor had always asked me to go to the BIH seminar, but I didn't see the need and didn't know about the BIH seminar. So when I came to the BIH seminar, I wasn't interested. I am in my fifties, and I am a kind of person who doesn't like listening to others. So, just like an observer, I was looking at others as they were praying and crying.

While I was watching others during the session, Dr. Kim said that we must forgive. When I heard the word "forgive," I felt like there was a heavy piece of rock inside my stomach. I was surprised and tried to figure out what it was. At that moment, the face of my late father came up.

I hated my father. The day my father passed away was the best day of my life. I felt so free when he passed away. For 40 years, he left home and never even called. Then, one day, he came back home. He was old and sick. My family didn't want to live with him. But I volunteered to take care of him. Whenever he felt better, he left home again and returned when he became sick. I resented him so much. But because he died, I thought there was nothing left between him and me.

When I felt the presence of this "piece of rock" and tried to figure out what it was, I realized that I haven't forgiven my father yet. Then, I also thought about my younger brother, who looked and acted like my father, so all my family hated him too. I also hated my brother whenever he visited me. I realized how I hated my father and brother.

I felt that two heavy pieces of rocks came out through my mouth and disappeared like a mist. I felt there was no more heaviness inside me. I had suffered from "stomachache" for so long that I couldn't sleep. But since that day, I have slept well without any pain.

CASE

Arrows in my heart and God's heart

I came to the BIH seminar with all the staff from my company as a part of our New Year retreat.

My husband came from a good Christian family. So I expected there wouldn't be trouble in our marriage. However, I was wrong. I asked God to let me know what to pray for during the seminar, and he let me think about "fear."

'Do I have fear? Of what?'

I realized that I had this fear of my husband. In general, he is kind and nice. But sometimes, he became abusive and swore at me when he got mad. I was afraid of him and got hurt. I saw my father-in-law beating his wife. I was afraid that my husband would eventually beat me like his father. During the prayer, I realized that I saw my father-in-law in my husband.

During the seminar, God showed me this particular scene. In the scene, my husband was swearing at me.

Words from his mouth became arrows coming to my heart. It was so vivid that I could feel how sharp they were. Arrows came and shot my heart. It was just a vision, but it was so real that I literally screamed. Then, I saw God next to me. The arrows were also shooting at the heart of God. He told me:

"Your husband shoots arrows not just to you, but also to me."

Just then, God removed arrows from my heart. They were covered with blood. God wiped the blood on my heart.

I felt sorry for my husband, but I decided to share it with others. I wanted others to know that verbal violence can hurt others as much as physical violence. I asked Rev. Joo and Dr. Kim to tell this story to others.

Today, people still stab Jesus with a knife, as they did two thousand years ago. Verbal violence against others stabs not only others but also God.

God was shot with an arrow, but he had stayed with me and my husband all the same.

SESSION 6

BE FILLED WITH THE HOLY SPIRIT

God keeps his words. God promised to let us be filled with the Holy Spirit. Ask God, and he will give you.

It is not for everyone, but only for God's children.

It is the most precious gift from God.

If you want to know and experience the Holy Spirit, You will.

PURPOSE OF THE SESSION

This session aims to help you know and experience the Holy Spirit.

The Holy Spirit breaks all the sins and bondages that hold us to allow us to experience true healing.

We can finally have a rich life when we are filled with the Holy Spirit.

Experience the Holy Spirit existing personally.
Experience the divine power of the Holy Spirit.

This session leads us to live our lives in the Holy Spirit.

BE FILLED WITH THE HOLY SPIRIT

1. Promise of Jesus

Jesus didn't leave us as orphans. The life of Christians is not that of followers. Jesus told people to stay in Jerusalem and wait to see God's words become true. Jesus told us to be baptized with the Holy Spirit, not by the water, as John the Baptist did to him.

> *But you will receive power when the Holy Spirit comes on you; and you will be my witnesses in Jerusalem, and in all Judea and Samaria, and to the ends of the earth.*
> *Acts 1:8*

Jesus told the apostles to be baptized with the Holy Spirit. Ten days later, they were filled with the Holy Spirit and were renewed.

All of them were filled with the Holy Spirit and began to speak in other tongues as the Spirit enabled them.
Acts 2:4

The apostles left the Sanhedrin, rejoicing because they had been counted worthy of suffering disgrace for the Name. Day after day, in the temple courts and from house to house, they never stopped teaching and proclaiming the good news that Jesus is the Messiah.
Acts 5:41-42

The apostles experienced immediate changes that didn't happen gradually. The apostles had shown weakness in following Jesus. However, they became whole new persons after being filled with the Holy Spirit.

2. Changes in Peter who betrayed Jesus

Peter deeply loved Jesus and left his work and family to follow him. However, because of his weakness and fear, he eventually betrayed Jesus. It is the weakness of humans before death.

However, Peter emerged at Pentecost as the lead apostle. He became so strong and loyal to Jesus that he gratefully accepted his execution for his belief.

The power that led to changes in Peter can't be described as a lesson or regret. He became a different person. It only took less than two months. The changes in him didn't happen by the will of Peter. It was only possible because he was filled with the Holy Spirit. This is the power we need as Christians.

3. Is the Pentecost a past event?

Acts 2 says something about the Pentecost where the Holy Spirit came. Was it the past event that happened only in the Bible? It was not a one-time event in the past. Today, we are still witnessing the power of the Holy Spirit.

Acts 8:14-25 talks about new believers receiving the Holy Spirit. The apostles in Jerusalem sent Peter and John to Samaria to pray for the new believers to receive the Holy Spirit. The church there had yet to experience baptism by the Holy Spirit. When they saw the presence of the Holy Spirit, they were astonished. They even offered Peter money to let them have an ability like the one he had shown, but Peter scolded them.

Throughout the Acts, we can find stories of people who sought to receive the Holy Spirit and eventually did so (Acts 10:44-48; Acts 19:1-7).

These stories in the Bible show that the presence of the Holy Spirit at the Pentecost was not just a past, one-time event. They showed that people who asked to have the Holy Spirit, whenever they were, actually received the Holy Spirit. The promise of God in Acts 1 is still valid today.

It is important to remember that receiving the Holy Spirit is not the same procedure as being a child of God.

It is a gift from God to people who have already received Jesus Christ.

4. Who is the Holy Spirit?

The Holy Spirit is the third person of the Trinity, which also includes Father God and his son, Jesus Christ. The Holy Spirit exists personally; it knows the thoughts of God (1 Corinthians 2:11), has emotions (Romans 15:30), and has the will to make choices (1 Corinthians 12:11).

5. Christians have to be baptized with the Holy Spirit and continue to be ruled by it

People have been in charge of their own lives. People have done whatever they want to do. When they become children of God, they need to learn a new way of life that has God as the master of their lives.

The apostle Paul knew that he was still in control. He knew his past involved struggling with the Holy Spirit to take control of his life.

> *What a wretched man I am! Who will rescue me from this body that is subject to death?*
> *Romans 7:24*

Paul found out that the only way to have victory in his life filled with struggles is to allow the Holy Spirit to take control of his life.

> *So I say, walk by the Spirit, and you will*
> *not gratify the desires of the flesh.*
> *Galatians 5:16*

6. Only the Holy Spirit can lead us into all the truth

> *But when he, the Spirit of truth, comes, he will*
> *guide you into all the truth. He will not speak*
> *on his own; he will speak only what he hears,*
> *and he will tell you what is yet to come.*
> *John 16:13*

When we receive the Holy Spirit and allow him to take control of us, we can experience things just like Jesus has said. The Holy Spirit lets God's child know the thoughts of God.

In other words, for us to know exactly what God thinks, we need the help of the Holy Spirit.

> *For who knows a person's thoughts except for their*
> *own spirit within them? In the same way no one*
> *knows the thoughts of God except the Spirit of God.*
> *1 Corinthians 2:11*

7. The Holy Spirit moved the human authors of the Bible to write about what he desired

Now, the Holy Spirit moves and writes words of the Bible inside us to understand what he desires.

> *All Scripture is God-breathed and is useful for teaching, rebuking, correcting and training in righteousness,*
> *2 Timothy 3:16*

To write God's words inside us, we need help from the Holy Spirit.

8. Why do some Christians fail to receive the Holy Spirit?

First, it is because they don't ask. They don't ask God because they don't know about God's promise, or even if they know, they are not confident that they will be heard. God promised that he would let us be filled with the Spirit. So we should ask God to do so.

> *If you then, though you are evil, know how to give good gifts to your children, how much more will your Father in heaven give the Holy Spirit to those who ask him!*
> *Luke 11:13*

Second, they don't see the need to have the Spirit. They

are not aware of the vulnerability they have. They don't feel uncomfortable with their habits and mindset from their old inner beings. They are not desperate to be changed. As a result, they remain Christians without a genuine relationship with God. They reject and don't accept the work of the Spirit (1 Corinthians 2:14).

Third, they seek the Holy Spirit for their self-interest. We should receive the Spirit to be a witness to Jesus Christ. Some people seek to have the Spirit for showing off to others or just out of curiosity. Some people ask God to be filled with the Spirit to be better than others, or to have extraordinary power for their self-interest. However, in this sense, they are offending God. Receiving the Spirit is not about having extraordinary power; rather, it is about giving the center of ourselves to the Spirit.

9. How should we receive the Holy Spirit?

i. Repent and receive Jesus Christ (Acts 2:38).
ii. If you recall any sins or a person you haven't repented for or forgiven, repent and decide to forgive.
iii. Ask God to let you be baptized with the Holy Spirit (Luke 11:13). After asking God, trust that you have been baptized. Praise God.
iv. Read what God told us (Ephesians 5:18) and acquaint yourselves with God's promise (1 John 5:14–15).
v. If you think you are weak, you are the one who needs to be filled with the Spirit.

If you sincerely believe that being filled with the Spirit is the will of God, you will receive the Spirit if you just ask God. Your prayer doesn't need to be long, fancy, or repetitive.

Receiving the Spirit doesn't necessarily let you speak in tongues or have abnormal experiences. In fact, you may not feel any difference. However, once you follow the steps and ask God, believe that you have received the Spirit. All gifts from God come through the channel of belief. If you decide to believe that you have received the Spirit, give thanks to and praise God.

10. Three things you should remember

Receiving the Spirit is not a one-time event.

If it was your first time receiving the Spirit, you just took the first step. You have to keep making choices to follow the Spirit. The outcome will vary depending on your next move.

You will see spiritual gifts in you from the Spirit.

These gifts include the word of knowledge, increased faith, gift of healing, prophecy, discernment of spirits, and interpretation of tongues. These spiritual gifts are given to you by the Spirit to be a witness. However, changes in your mind in relation to your relationship with God should always be prioritized before the gift.

Understand the difference between baptism with the Holy Spirit and being filled with the Spirit.

Being born again happens once when we receive Jesus. The baptism with the Holy Spirit is also a one-time event that happens once in our lives. However, being filled with the Holy Spirit is not an event, but more like a status that you should aim to keep in your entire life. Life filled with the Holy Spirit refers to a life that follows the Spirit, not our own will or thoughts.

Once you are baptized with the Spirit, you have to maintain your life to be filled with it. Baptism with the Holy Spirit initiates a journey with the Spirit. We should keep our lives filled throughout our relationship with the Spirit, which can be strengthened when we listen and obey the Spirit.

Jesus showed the life that walks with the Spirit. He listened and followed what the Spirit told him to do. The greatest sin among Christians is controlling their lives and doing whatever they want to do without listening to the Spirit.

CASE

I was about to give up being a Christian

I am a professional soldier. People say I am a proud soldier. However, I lost confidence in myself. In particular, I was not happy about myself as a Christian. I was disappointed in my belief in God and my life as a Christian.

I felt exhausted. Before joining the military, I was confident and proud of myself as a Christian. However, as the years passed, I lost faith and joy in God.

I told a Christian counselor how I had struggled to get my faith back.

She replied, "We are weak. That's why Jesus told us to receive the Spirit."

"I don't get it. I thought I had already received the Spirit when I received Jesus. Why should I need to receive the Spirit?"

I asked her. Again, she replied,

"The Spirit is already in you, of course. Rather, it would be more precise to say that you are in the Spirit. However, this doesn't mean things are done. Because we are in the Spirit, we should ask the Spirit to help and give us power. I also struggled to get my faith back by myself. I prayed and read the Bible over and over. However, it didn't make any changes. It made me frustrated. I was about to give up being a Christian. But I realized that I didn't follow the steps."

"What step?"

I didn't understand what she meant by that, but she looked confident, so I listened to her.

"I thought I needed to pray and feel faithful to meet God. However, I was wrong. Rather, I need to meet God because I don't feel faithful and can't pray. If we stand before God and feel empty, God gives us the power to pray. Before making any effort to do something with our beliefs or emotions, the first step should be getting help from the Holy Spirit. I didn't know. I always took the wrong step. So I always failed. What do you think? Do you feel the same?"

Her experience gave me insight. It spoke to me. Then, I asked her,

"So if I receive the Holy Spirit even though I don't feel anything now, can I be faithful and feel God?"

"Yes. What's important is that you accept your weaknesses and that you can't keep your faith by yourself. You don't want to be a hypocrite, and you know you are weak. That's what makes you scared."

"That's correct. I hate being a hypocrite, but I am not

confident about myself. I am too weak."

"That's why you need the power. The power that will allow you to have faith and be a Christian in every circumstance. The Holy Spirit baptizes us to give power. I think it will solve your issue."

"But.. I am not ready…"

"Ready for what?"

"I don't know. But shouldn't I do something before receiving the Spirit? Like wash my face or... something?"

"You never can be ready to receive the Spirit. We don't have any power, even to be ready. The only thing we can do is accept and know our weaknesses. I think you are ready, as you already know your weaknesses."

I was speechless. I sat on my knees with her. At the same time, I was scared. What if nothing happens? So I asked her,

"But…please know that I am not a person who usually gets miracles or spiritual experiences..."

To this, she answered,

"What we are doing here is not to have some gifts or special experiences. We just ask the Spirit what you need. The key is his will. Does the Holy Spirit want you to receive the Spirit? If you ask the same thing the Spirit wants, he will give it to you."

I agreed with her. I thought it was biblically correct. So I said a simple prayer with her. I asked God to give me the power to be faithful and continue to be Christian. I also asked him to let me speak in tongues.

The prayer wasn't long; it was short and straightforward. But I had faith. I just spoke out and tried to speak in tongues with belief. I listened to myself speaking out weird things I didn't understand. I was stunned. Everything was so easy and natural.

'Was it this easy?!' I thought to myself. I didn't even need to shout or repeat anything. God answered me just like that. A month later, I came back to meet the counselor. I told her what happened in my life.

"So first, now I know that I had the wrong idea about the Spirit. I was not comfortable when people talked about the Spirit. I was also afraid to receive the Holy Spirit. I thought it's something that made people scream, change their voice, or do weird things, but I was wrong about all of that. The Holy Spirit I met was so gentle, calm, and respected me as an individual.

Second, I now have this clear idea about heaven. Before, when people talked about heaven, I just had a vague idea or image and didn't feel it was real, but now I do.

Finally, I feel that something has changed in me. I always had this clump in my heart. I felt like I was stuck to something, but I didn't know what it was. Since the day I met the Holy Spirit, that clump has disappeared. I don't know how to tell this to others or describe it. Now, I am full of hope."

Since then, I have been living a Christian life with confidence. I feel the power of the Spirit, not mine. I now know how to rely on God. I have given my life to God.

CASE

What changed me was not the thirty years of education but three days of Bible study

I have attended church since I was nine. Now, I am teaching children. I have been told spiritual things through my mother since I was young. Unfortunately, most of them were about demons and evil spirits, and as a result, I was always afraid of spiritual experience.

I didn't want to be like my mother, a Christian focusing too much on the spiritual aspect. So I tried to keep myself away from spiritual experiences. I did what good Christians would do, except for those spiritual parts. It worked for me.

A few years ago, there was a time in Korea when people were overwhelmed by rapture. Flyers were spreading, talking about the second coming of Jesus. I knew they were a cult. However, I questioned myself. 'Will I be caught up to meet God when it happens?' I wasn't confident enough to answer "Yes." That's when I realized that the past years of my life as a Christian were worthless. I knew God was real. However, I wasn't sure about his love. 'Does God really love me?' I wanted to be sure about this question.

I consulted a counselor about this issue. She told me about the Holy Spirit. I followed what she suggested. I read Biblical verses about the Spirit and agreed on the need to receive the Spirit. She asked me to pray.

Because I had never had a spiritual experience, I had doubts, even while praying with her. The prayer was short and straightforward, but I received the Spirit. I spoke in tongues. I was overwhelmed with indescribable joy. I came back to my office and started to pray in tongues. It was hard for me to pray for more than five minutes. But that day, I prayed for over two hours with a loud voice. Someone knocked on my office. My colleague was standing there wondering what was happening in my office. Since then, I have made it clear what type of Christian I should be.

Now, I have no hesitation in telling others that I am Christian. I want to know God more. I know that the spiritual world is not all about evil and demons but is the world controlled by God.

I see changes in me. I have a doctoral degree in education, but I now see that receiving the Holy Spirit can be a much better way to change people than education in one's lifetime. The ultimate purpose of education would be to bring about this kind of change in people.

SESSION 7

THE BONDS THAT KEEP YOU AWAY FROM YOUR TRUE FATHER

To be free from the lonesomeness and anxiety that cause disease and illness, we need to meet God as our true father.

PURPOSE OF THE SESSION

We can't have an intimate relationship with God if we have the wrong perception of him. The emptiness felt by humans cannot be filled without a relationship with God.

People who feel such emptiness can be considered spiritual and emotional orphans. They may have a biological father or think they know God. However, if they can't truly feel the love of God, they will live and feel like orphans.

If you see your child being nervous and afraid of others, you may feel very upset. Likewise, God feels sad and upset when we act and feel like a child without our parents. Simply put, God is the father, and we are his children.

The current session aims to help you understand why it is difficult to see God as the father. Armed with such information, it helps you recognize God as your true father.

Jesus said he is the way. Here, "way" does not mean the destination. It means the path that leads us to the destination. Then, where does Jesus want to take us? The answer is that he wants to take us to the father.

Jesus wants us to know who Father God is and to have a relationship with him like he does. If someone genuinely feels God as the true father who is friendly and deeply loves us, it means this person truly believes God's word in his or her mind. The person is free from fear and concerns. However, many Christians have the wrong image of God in their minds and don't feel God as a friendly father. They pray and go to church, but they still feel like orphans. Jesus doesn't want us to stand alone outside his home. He wants to take us inside his home, where the father is.[46]

Why do we have the wrong image of Father God?

---

[46] Jesus comforted his disciples. "Do not let your hearts be troubled. You believe in God; believe also in me. My Father's house has many rooms; if that were not so, would I have told you that I am going there to prepare a place for you?"(John 14:1-2); Jesus answered, "I am the way and the truth and the life. No one comes to the Father except through me." (John 14:6)

THE BONDS THAT KEEP YOU AWAY FROM YOUR TRUE FATHER

1. The relationship with a human father shapes the relationship with God the Father

A human father figure has the most significant impact on shaping the image of God the Father. We have a relationship with our human father when we are young, though it may not be strong and mature enough. The experience with our human father and our emotions with him shape the basis of our personality. It determines how we see the world. It impacts how our minds see things.

What are the symptoms of not being able to see God right?

The most common symptom is anxiety without reasonable cause. People with these symptoms are always expecting something bad to happen. Their minds are controlled by anxiety, such that they can't be happy when something goes well. They always anticipate that something bad will happen. They constantly live in fear that their lives will ultimately fail.

This anxiety in their minds leads to emptiness inside. When Christians experience this anxiety and emptiness, they continuously feel guilty. They are always nervous, and this is a symptom of trying to protect ourselves.

1) A good father

If people have a good father, it would be relatively easy to see God as a father. God chose to send us to this world as babies, not as adults. God also allowed us to be part of a family so that we would be cared for. By being part of a family, we learn the concept of a mother and a father and what devoted love means. Through this experience, we gained a better understanding of God's love and him as "Father God."

However, a good father can still hurt his child. Yet, getting hurt is not entirely determined by the act of a father, but by how a child interprets it and the circumstances in which it is committed. Let's say a father left his home to find a better job. He lives away from his family to make more money for them. In this situation, he doesn't mean to hurt his child. However, his child may feel abandoned or even hurt because of an incorrect interpretation. Fortunately, as long as there's a good relationship between the father and his child, these wrong interpretations can be solved. In this case, it won't be an issue for a child to know Father God.

2) A father who easily gets mad

If people are raised by a father who gets mad quickly, they not only become a person with anger, but also with the wrong image of God. They often imagine God as a being who is ready to discipline. They think God will judge and punish their behaviors rather than be generous and forgiving.

Thus, these people are always nervous about making mistakes. They can't accept their mistakes and those of others. However, God is not waiting for us to make mistakes. He is generous and patient with us when we are wrong and experience failure. He doesn't get frustrated with us.

He heals the brokenhearted and binds up their wounds. This is what God is like. Yet people can't believe it when they are blind to see God.

> *The Lord upholds all who fall and lifts*
> *up all who are bowed down.*
> Psalms 145:14

3) An emotionally distant father

Distant fathers don't really express their feelings or emotions. They don't laugh, cry, or smile. They are outside the family and try to control them from that position. They go to work early in the morning and come back late. They don't spend time with their children. When they are home, they don't have deep conversations with the members. Thus, children with this type of father face challenges in terms of sharing their feelings and emotions with other people.

When these children grow up, they don't know how to have relationships or conversations with their own children. Hence, they tend to do the same when they meet God.

"God, I will do this job for you. God. I will give this to you."

Their relationship with God is religious and abstract. They talk to God only about the big things in their lives. They don't share their everyday emotions and events with God. They don't think God cares about their daily feelings or minor issues.

However, over 90 percent of our lives are made up of small and minor issues. If we can't talk to God about small things in our lives, we can't share most of our lives as well. A child who can't share his ordinary daily life with his father feels lonely and may find a sinful way to solve this lonesomeness.

4) A weak father

A family with a weak father often has a strong mother who controls issues in the family. These mothers are often breadwinners who take control of the family's financial affairs. Therefore, children discuss everything mainly with their mothers. Children with a weak father can't rely on themselves and on God as well. This type of family does not follow the order of a normal family by God. Therefore, it naturally damages children.

Sons with weak fathers often grow up and become as weak as their fathers. They are likely to hate women in power who are like their mothers. However, ironically, they often get married to a woman like their mother.

In particular, they get married to a woman in control and then develop repressed anger toward her. In that case, their children might get hurt.

Meanwhile, daughters with weak fathers get furious when their husbands lack confidence or show weakness like their fathers. If they feel that they can't trust their husbands, they will then try to control their lives.

Children with weak fathers often become fearful. However, God is almighty and gentle. We can rely entirely on him because he is the one with the power that lasts forever.

5) No father

Children who don't have a father grow up not having an actual concept or image of a father because they don't have experience. Divorce, overseas dispatch or work, or death can take a father away from his children. Thus, children with no father find it challenging to trust God's involvement in their lives or even to have a relationship with him.

However, God is always with us. He is not far away. In fact, he has been with us since the day we were born. We have to meet our God the Father, not only in heaven but also in this world.

6) An alcoholic father

Children with alcoholic fathers face severe emotional pain. They don't want to feel ashamed of their parents, yet an alcoholic father continuously makes his children feel mad, frustrated, and ashamed. Children feel guilty when they see their fathers. As they feel guilty about judging their father, they don't share their emotional pain or embarrassment with others. Instead, they try to neglect and bury these feelings.

Unfortunately, the mood of the drunken father determines the mood of the family. For example, no matter how sad or tired the children are, the drunken father wakes them up at night and asks them to sing. Sometimes, when the father does not feel so good when he is drunk, he shouts at his children for no reason. The feelings and emotions of his children are neglected and disrespected. Thus, as they grow up, children become guardians against their fathers. Sometimes, they even need to protect their mothers from their drunken fathers.

The typical symptom that people share when they have a drunken father is a feeling of insecurity. As their feelings aren't respected when they are young, they grow up not knowing how to care for or respect their own feelings. They tend to ignore their feelings and follow others. Moreover, they tend to intervene with others' business. It makes their mind "overcrowded" and busy.

When they become Christians, they are devoted to being good Christians. They don't share or even try to show their feelings or emotions with God. They are only ready to listen to and follow God's order. They don't expect God to care about their feelings, like their father. They only focus on serving God. Yet, ultimately, they don't care for or feel God's love.

However, we are not servants of God; rather, we are the children of God. He cares deeply about how we feel. He respects our emotions. As he respects each of us, he considers us his precious and unique children.

7) A father who has abandoned his child

Surprisingly, many fathers abandon their children. For instance, some parents send their children to orphanages. When children feel abandoned, they tend to give up on themselves as well. It makes them vulnerable to sinning later in their lives. However, God said that he would never abandon us.

> *Though my father and mother forsake me, the Lord will receive me.*
> *Psalms 27:10*

8) A father who feels ashamed of his child

Some fathers feel ashamed of their children. Due to their reputation or expectations, they may be disappointed and/or angry with their children. They continuously ask their children to be someone they expect them to be. Children born outside of marriage or under specific circumstances can also feel the same. In this case, a father loves his child, but acts like he doesn't in front of others.

However, God never feels ashamed of us, regardless of our sins. Jesus led us to be his siblings. He is also not ashamed of us.[47] God loves us in public and has never

---

[47] Both the one who makes people holy and those who are made holy are of the same family. So Jesus is not ashamed to call them brothers and sisters. (Hebrews 2:11)

hesitated to say, "I love you. I am your father. You are my child." He publicly announced this to the world and the universe. He even said this before we repented—when we were still dirty and weak.

9) Abusive father

Unfortunately, the most traumatic cases that hurt people's souls happen inside a family. Every day, we see on the news acts of sexual violence, physical violence, human trafficking, or even murder that happened within a family. Satan may use dysfunctional families to destroy us. However, God also made a family to bless us.

Children may suffer from fatal damage inside when their fathers harm them, and none of the therapies or programs in the world can heal such damage. Only God's love can heal them, as God is the father of our spirit.

Furthermore, God never takes advantage of nor harms his children. Everything that we have in our lives is from him, and he continues to provide us with what we need.

We are disciplined to be better off. It is not a punishment. God doesn't have the habit of punishing us because he is mad. God doesn't turn his back on us. He takes care of us and raises us as his children. He also gave his life for us.

2. Grudges against God keep us from being closer to him

Sometimes, when we have troubles in our lives, we blame God. This situation pushes us to harbor grudges against God. Troubles in our lives also become troubles in our spirits. Satan has the ability to tell us lies and poison our minds when we are in a difficult time in our lives.

"God didn't protect me from bad things. He is punishing me. He doesn't care about me. If he cared, this wouldn't have happened to me. Maybe people are faking God's love."

It is easy to blame God the almighty when we become desperate. No one can explain why God allowed some things to happen. We should believe his words rather than keep asking, "Why, God?"

> *Don't be deceived, my dear brothers and sisters. Every good and perfect gift is from above, coming down from the Father of the heavenly lights, who does not change like shifting shadows.*
> *James 1:16-17*

Satan keeps telling us lies about God, convincing us that he doesn't care about the pains of humans. Listening to these lies makes us blind, so God tells us to avoid such deceptions. He tells us to be thankful in every circumstance, even though we can't understand. He promised that he would work for the good in all things.

> *And we know that in all things God works*
> *for the good of those who love him, who have*
> *been called according to his purpose.*
> Romans 8:28

The Bible contains stories of people who choose to trust God regardless of hardships in their lives. We are not responsible for some of the troubles in our lives. However, we are fully responsible for our responses and choices as we go through life's challenges.

God feels bad when we are desperate. He cares deeply about how we feel. He is not cold or insensitive.[48]

When you feel desperate, God is not just up there watching you. He is right next to you.

3. Inherited bondages and curses keep us from being with God

Fraud, stealing, cursing, drinking alcohol, bawdiness, lying, and fortunetelling are some forms of bondage that lead to sin. The Bible says such bondage is inherited over four generations.[49]

---

[48] As a father has compassion on his children, so the Lord has compassion on those who fear him; for he knows how we are formed, he remembers that we are dust. (Psalms 103:13-14)

[49] You shall not bow down to them or worship them; for I, the Lord your God, am a jealous God, punishing the children for the sin of the parents to the third and fourth generation of those who hate me. (Exodus 20:5)

In the family, we may be blinded from seeing God due to bondages, such as magic, bawdiness, worshiping idols, having diseases, or depression. Fortunately, Jesus—through his Cross—breaks all those bondages. We need to break any sinful bondages in our families, including those inherited from our parents. We have to overcome these in the name of Jesus.

When Nehemiah prayed for his people, he found bondages between their ancestors and himself. He repented and eventually defeated these bondages.[50]

We should break bondages in our families if there are any. There is no reason why these should be passed on to our children.

4. Fetal memory impacts one's relationship with God

Many cultures value prenatal care. The bottom line of prenatal care is based on the idea that a fetus is a human who needs to be respected. The Bible shows that a fetus already has emotions and even the ability to think. For example, Elizabeth's baby was happy in her womb when Mary visited her.[51]

---

[50] Let your ear be attentive and your eyes open to hear the prayer your servant is praying before you day and night for your servants, the people of Israel. I confess the sins we Israelites, including myself and my father's family, have committed against you. We have acted very wickedly toward you. We have not obeyed the commands, decrees and laws you gave your servant Moses. (Nehemiah 1:6-7)

[51] See Luke 1:39-44

Experts have also offered scientific grounds that support this idea. According to a study, the mother's mind and emotions are shared with the unborn baby in her womb.[52] Scientists have further shown that a person's experience in the womb impacts one's character and personality later in life. Moreover, a child with parents who argue often has a 2.5 times higher chance of mental and physical illness and a five times higher chance of being temperamental than a child with parents who don't argue.[53]

However, once we are born, we can't go back to our old state. The good news is that God can fix things that we used to have while still inside the womb.

During the BIH seminar, many people saw how they were and knew how they felt when they were a fetus. They discovered how those experiences in the womb had impacted their lives. They witnessed how the Holy Spirit healed the wounds they had from the womb.

5. Lies that keep us from God

"Once I believe in Jesus, my past won't affect my life anymore."

Some people think the past is gone when they become Christians. In particular, they expect the experiences, sins,

---

[52] Verney, Thomas (1988) *The Secret Life of the Unborn Child.* Dell Publishing Company.

[53] Ibid.

and wounds from the past to no longer have the power to impact their lives. However, they soon found out that it was wrong. When we meet Jesus, our spirit changes, but this doesn't mean that our minds and bodies do the same.

Being a Christian means that, now, we are on the right track to being renewed. Our minds need fundamental change. There should be a step we need to take to be free from the past. If some people say that there's no need to go through the past as they already believe in Jesus, they are ignorant of psychological areas and are not deeply faithful. In this case, they are like disbelievers who are ignorant of spiritual areas.

"My emotional issues will be fixed if I become more knowledgeable of the Bible."

Emotional issues, personality disorders, and vulnerability to sin are often developed during childhood. These are habits that can't be easily fixed or corrected.

To cure diseases, we need to be diagnosed first so that a proper treatment regimen can be designed for us. Likewise, to cure old habits in us, we need to follow the steps prescribed by the Holy Spirit.

"I feel bad and guilty to blame my parents for my wrongdoings."

> "I feel like I am blaming my parents if I try to find the causes of my wrongdoings from my childhood."

> "I am embarrassed to share about my childhood and my parents with others."

Unfortunately, an individual's relationships with his/her parents are the primary causes of wounds inside a person. Therefore, it is difficult not to think about your relationship with your parents during the BIH seminar. Whether they are still alive or have already passed away, we can truly say that our parents have made a lasting impact on us.

The BIH seminar features sessions that encourage participants to go through how their parents behaved and treated them through prayers. This step is not about blaming your parents. Instead, the goal of such an exercise is to understand any lingering wounds inside you. It is the first step you need to take to cure your inner wounds. Once you know their causes, you will feel secure and relieved. It will give you the power to take the next step.

6. What is the truth that sets us free?

Looking into the behaviors of your parents is not the same as blaming or criticizing them.

It is an essential step to take to bring restoration to the family. Neglecting or minimizing pain in us doesn't mean the pain will disappear. Instead, it will leave a larger stain inside us.

Forgiveness is the way to love your parents. Hiding is not.

God encourages us to respect our parents. When we truly know their weaknesses, we are empowered to accept and love them.

The Holy Spirit allows us to discover our parents' weaknesses. It is not to blame them, but to let us know who we are.

Knowing the weakness and mindset of parents allows us to realize their influence on us. It is the first step that should be taken to set us free from sinful bondage. It leads us to stand on our own feet. We can truly rely on God only when we gain independence from our parents in a healthy way.

7. How can we remove the false image of Father God from us?

Jeremiah prayed for the recovery of their people. During the prayer, he found that there were inherited sins and habits in his family. He repented and was determined to break them (Jeremiah 9:2). Specifically, rather than blaming his parents or ancestors, he admitted that he allowed himself to accept the sinful habits and then chose to repent for these sins.

What Jeremiah did can serve as a good lesson for us: He stood humble before God and was desperate to meet him. Meanwhile, these are the steps that should be followed:

i. Accept that the troubles you have with your parents have kept you away from God.
ii. Ask God and inform him about what you think of him and why. Share with him all the details of any experiences you recall during prayer.
iii. If your parents have hurt your feelings or your heart, forgive them and express your love. Even if your parents have passed away, forgive them anyway and speak out you love them.
iv. Pray in the name of Jesus so that you can break the inherited sins, habits, and bondages in your family. Ask the Holy Spirit to intervene. The name of Jesus can make miracles.

CASE

God hung out with me at the empty playground

My father was no longer around before I was born. My mother got married and left me when I was young. Thus, I was raised by my grandmother. I didn't know how to express my feelings and thoughts. I barely talked. At school, I didn't pay the tuition until the school called my family and told them that I was suspended.

I met my husband at a church. He was a pastor who cared for and loved me like he was my parent. His love made me forget about my parents and my painful childhood. For twenty years of marriage, I have never shared my childhood or my parents with my husband. He didn't ask me either. I didn't think it would impact my relationship with God.

I came to the BIH seminar and had a chance to read Psalms 139. It was about God who made me in my mother's womb, and at once, I felt very unfamiliar with the experience of calling God "Father." I served at our church with my husband, I was certain about God as a guide in my life. However, I didn't think of God as my father.

It was the first time I realized this. So I started to think about why I did so.

During the session, there was a case of a father who was not with his children. When I heard the case, I felt something heavy in my heart.

'I didn't have any memory of my father. Then, which father figure do I have? Can God do something for me, who never had a father?'

Then, I recalled an unexpected memory. I was about seven years old at that time, and I was sitting at the playground in school, playing by myself. It was late afternoon, and the sun was already setting. No one was there. I played Tom Tiddler's ground. I played two roles to feel like I was with a friend. A guard at school approached me and told me that I should go. I didn't know where to go. So I was standing alone at the playground.

I didn't understand why I recalled this memory. It was just an ordinary day in my childhood — nothing special. But then, I felt something heavy and frustrating. I prayed and asked God, "God, what do you want?"

Then, he showed me the scene again. I was standing alone at the playground, but this time, God was coming to me and playing Tom Tiddler's ground with me.

We had so much fun together. For the first time, I felt the joy of a child playing with her father. I couldn't stop crying since then. I cried over and over, even when I came back home.

I also recalled other memories of my childhood when I prayed. I felt as if many closed doors inside me were opened. Healing was occurring inside me and brought drastic changes to my relationships with others.

The first change was in my relationship with my mother. God told me,

"You listened to other people gossiping about your father. You saw your mother getting married and leaving you. Since then, you have abandoned everyone, even yourself."

He was right. I didn't have any relationship with anyone. I didn't even have a relationship with my grandmother who raised me.

Thus, I decided to visit my mother, whom my husband had never met before. She left me when I was young, and when I visited her, she was already an old lady. I am now a middle-aged woman, but when I met her, I cried like a child.

Since then, I felt that all the emotions and feelings dead inside me have been revived. I feel like I am becoming a normal person.

The most significant change is my relationship with God.

Now, I feel and recognize God as my father. Words in the Bible speak to my heart. Before, I barely cried, but now, whenever I think about God playing Tom Tiddler's ground with me at the playground, I can't stop crying.

People in my church also changed after witnessing my transformation. They shared their stories with their small groups in the church. Since then, there has been a continuous flow of healing and blessings in the church.

CASE

My food allergy has disappeared

I was born into a Christian family. I have been a good Christian all my life. However, I often had troubles with my mother. That's why, when I was at the BIH seminar, I prayed for my relationship with my mother. During the prayer, I thought about the session, talking about a hole inside of us.

The speaker said, "Getting hurt creates a hole inside us. Most times, people ignore and cover that hole. However, the Holy Spirit goes into the hole to heal us."

I asked God, "God, are there any holes inside me? If there are, please show me, and please heal me."

Then, I saw a vision. It was a fetus. I thought I was just distracted. So I prayed.

"God, is it you showing me a fetus? I don't get it. If it's you, please let me understand."

"It is you."

I felt like God was telling me. Then I saw that the fetus

was furious and screaming, so I asked again, "God, why is this fetus angry?"

"You hate your mother and despise your father."

Suddenly, I recalled the sins I made. I thought I didn't have any sin to confess, but I realized that I had justified myself in committing sins. I repented in tears. I asked God to forgive me. I thought about the Cross.

'Jesus died on the Cross to save me, a sinner! Jesus forgave me. Then I should forgive my parents too...'

I wanted to forgive my parents, but I wasn't sure what to forgive.

"God, I forgive my parents. I forgive everything about my parents."

It was a short prayer, but I felt like it had significant weight on what I was trying to do. Then I thought about the fetus again, and I saw that he was falling asleep peacefully. I saw a tear on his face—it was a tear of gratefulness.

Later, I had a chance to talk with my mother, who told me about the time when she was pregnant. After this conversation, I was assured again that it was God who showed me the scene.

Before she had me, she had a miscarriage. Then, when she became pregnant with me, my father was dispatched to the other side of the country, so she was by herself for five months. One time, food had run out, and my mother couldn't get any help from her parents and siblings, as they had severe financial issues at that time. My mother was full of anger and hatred against my father, and she seemed to have passed on this emotion to me—a fetus in her womb.

I also discovered that I developed food allergies when my mother was pregnant. When she had me, she didn't have anything to eat. There was a peach farm in her neighborhood. So she only ate peaches for five months. As a result, I developed a terrible allergy to peaches. I couldn't even touch my children if they ate peaches. Though my family loved peaches, I got mad whenever I saw peaches at home. One day after the BIH seminar, I ate a plate of salad at a table, and my wife was amazed and asked me.

"Are you okay?"

"What do you mean?"

"There were peaches in that salad."

I was surprised that I didn't have allergic symptoms. That summer, I ate a lot of peaches. So did my family.

For the past 40 years of my life as a Christian, I had never thought there was a deep hole inside me. I didn't even know that I despised my parents. I thought I had a good Christian life. The Holy Spirit let me know what was inside of me, and because of him, I was healed from the "holes" I had when I was a fetus. I believe no one can make this happen without the help of the Spirit.

SESSION 8

THE SPIRITUAL WARFARE INSIDE ME

Christians who believe in God should be aware of the presence of evil spirits. Satan itself, along with demons and ghosts, continues to harm and deceive us. We are in spiritual warfare, and it is taking place inside us. To win, we should be aware of this ongoing internal war.

PURPOSE OF THE SESSION

What we can't see rules over what we can see. Thus, people who can control the blinded world can control the world that we can see.

Christians are soldiers of God. The enemies attack us not through guns and missiles; rather, they attack our vulnerability and weakness. Therefore, to win the spiritual war, we must be able to strengthen ourselves by overcoming our weaknesses.

To have the power to win this spiritual warfare, we should prepare our minds in two steps:

First, we should heal the weakness inside us that the enemy attempts to attack. Second, we should be aware of the lies and deceptions of Satan.

These two steps help us confront the enemies and win the war.

Christians face such a spiritual battle every day. God told us how to win the battle.

Finally, be strong in the Lord and in his mighty power. Put on the full armor of God, so that you can take your stand against the devil's schemes. For our struggle is not against flesh and blood, but against the rulers, against the authorities, against the powers of this dark world, and against the spiritual forces of evil in the heavenly realms. Therefore put on the full armor of God, so that when the day of evil comes, you may be able to stand your ground, and after you have done everything, to stand.

Ephesians 6:10-13

THE SPIRITUAL WARFARE INSIDE ME

1. Whether we care or not, whether we are ready or not, Christians are in a spiritual warfare. Why can't we avoid this battle?

If an individual doesn't believe in God, then there is no battle within him, because it is likely that Satan has already taken over. However, when a person decides to receive the spirit of God, a severe battle takes place inside him. This is the battle between the spirit of God and the old sinful spirit that has controlled the past. The life of each Christian is a place where the evil spirit and the spirit of God confront each other.

Satan takes control over the world through the sins people make. Christians who follow God's words are a severe threat to Satan. If Christians neglect this spiritual battle, we can't use any power of God, and we will not win.

2. Two extreme misunderstandings about the spiritual sphere

There are two common misunderstandings about the spiritual sphere. One is denial, and the other is giving too much attention to it.

Extreme denial

Some people don't admit the presence of the evil spirit. They think evil spirits are irrelevant in their lives if they don't pay attention to them. They don't feel comfortable when people talk about demon possessions in churches. Sometimes, they even think that demon possession and spiritual battle are forms of heathenism. They think that this is no longer their business, as Jesus had already defeated Satan two thousand years ago.

However, knowing and admitting the presence of Satan is not the cause that leads us to spiritual warfare. Regardless of the current situation, we are in spiritual warfare. Not being interested in the evil spirit doesn't mean that the evil spirit is not interested in us. They keep their eyes on us and prepare to destroy God's children at opportune times. We have to know thoroughly about the evil spirit as we know God. The truth will set us free and make us strong.

Too much attention

Some people pay too much attention to the evil spirit. These people often experience anxiety and fear. Thus, they tend to blame the evil spirit for anything bad that happens in their lives, such as car accidents, an argument with their spouse, being sick, and so on. For this reason, they always put their energy into confronting Satan. Sometimes, they even blame Satan for their own mistakes, selfishness, and sins, fully avoiding their responsibility for such wrongdoings.

At the same time, some people think of themselves as spiritually gifted people. They brag about their ability to defeat Satan. They are looking for people or events to show off their spiritual gifts. However, spiritual warfare is not all about defeating Satan. Defeating Satan is only a part of it.

3. How can you prepare yourself for spiritual warfare?

We can prepare for spiritual warfare by focusing on Jesus Christ and the Gospel of the Cross. Our minds focus on what we are afraid of. We feel afraid when we don't have full information about an enemy. Thus, to win this spiritual warfare and be empowered and free from fear, we should know about the enemy.

When we experience some kind of spiritual event, we should not determine the cause by asking ourselves or even Satan. We should ask God only. This is the only way to protect us from the fear of being attacked by the evil spirit.

Furthermore, we should know who we are in God. Satan attacks people who lack confidence in God's love. Thus, we should firmly believe that we are the children of God. Then, we can use the power of God to defeat Satan.

4. Who is Satan?

Who is Satan?

Satan is a creature of God. Therefore, it can't compete with God. Satan has never been a god of the world. It has never owned the world God created. However, it interrupted the path of Jesus Christ and manipulated people to kill Jesus on the Cross. It was only possible, as Satan manipulated the minds of people who were given the ruling power by God (Romans 6:16).

Satan uses humans, whom God loves the most, as instruments. However, Jesus has broken every strategy of Satan on the Cross (John 12:31). If you don't believe Satan's lies and are a Christian believing in God's love, you are living proof that Satan's strategies have been overpowered.

The one who does what is sinful is of the devil because the devil has been sinning from the beginning. The reason the Son of God appeared was to destroy the devil's work.
1 John 3:8

What happened to Satan?

God didn't intend to create Satan as the evil spirit. In fact, God created Satan as the most beautiful angel among all angels. However, Satan desired to have God's authority and throne and rule the universe. In its arrogance, Satan rebelled against God and fell from the heavens (Isaiah 14:12–15). It was Satan who implanted this idea into Adam and Eve and destroyed them. This idea of Satan—the desire to possess God's authority—still lives in people.

Satan's character

Satan's character is the opposite of God's. The cruelty of Satan has been shown all over the world. Tortures, medical experiments on a living body, violence, rape and murder in a family, slavery, and so on, show the cruelty of Satan. Satan uses all kinds of tools to spread his ideas to people. Furthermore, through music, film, art, books, etc., Satan spreads his ideas and characters to all kinds of media platforms and channels. People are exposed to its ideas and "images." The exposure of children to violent video games and films has resulted in a number of tragic crimes. Horrifying crimes and the cruelty of humans show the character of Satan.

What does Satan see in humans?

> *Therefore rejoice, you heavens and you who dwell in them! But woe to the earth and the sea, because the devil has gone down to you! He is filled with 'fury', because he knows that his time is short.*
> *Revelation 12:12*

The word "fury" above is translated as thymas in the original Greek language. It refers to an overwhelming rage coupled with a deep grudge. This is how Satan feels about God. With thymas, Satan searches for God's children and attempts to destroy them. Satan is waiting for the moment when Christians become vulnerable to crises and pains in their lives. This is a crucial reason why we should remove the bitter root inside us because Satan uses these as channels with which to attack us.

What is Satan's role in the world?

God created the world for humans and gave them all the authority to rule over the world. However, humans left God and lost their authority to rule the world. In doing so, humans handed over their authority to Satan. Satan leads the world by spreading its ideas to people using the authority handed over from them. As mentioned previously, this idea is revealed through culture, politics, religion, the environment, science, and so on. Satan does not physically exist, but can only work in the spiritual sphere. It deceives and manipulates people in the spiritual sphere so that they can serve as puppets who will do what it wants them to do in the physical world. Satan destroys beauty in humans and in the environments that God created.

5. Spiritual warfare for Christians

Whether you want it or not, there's a war inside you if you are Christian. Your thoughts and the words you utter show whether you have won or lost the battle. God wants us to win this spiritual war, and we can. However, we can also be defeated, but the outcome is up to us because the war is happening inside us (James 1:14–15).

Minds are the center of the spiritual warfare

God tells us his thoughts, and we use our minds to receive and understand these thoughts. Satan is also telling its thoughts in the same way. This was how Satan was able to prompt Judas to betray Jesus (John 13:2). Satan uses several ways to spread his thoughts inside us.

Cursing

Satan uses the act of cursing through family members, friends, fortunetellers, or neighbors to hold our minds hostage throughout our lives.

Suggestions

Peter suggested that Jesus not die on the Cross. Jesus knew where Peter got the idea and defeated Satan. Although Peter suggested the idea to Jesus, it was actually Satan's idea. Satan also suggested that Judas betray Jesus. Like Satan did to Peter and Judas, it makes suggestions to you as well. Unfortunately, it is not easy to be aware of these suggestions from the evil spirit. In everyday life, we get suggestions from Satan:

"Just tell her lies. She won't find out."

"How about stealing it? No one is watching you."

"Why don't you just do it? It is not a big deal. God will forgive you anyway."

If we follow these suggestions, we soon feel guilty and are defeated in the spiritual battle mentioned earlier. These suggestions are from Satan. They are attacks made by Satan. Unfortunately, Christians often believe they themselves made those suggestions, not Satan. When they realize the truth, they feel guilty and blame themselves. This leads them to a path away from God.

Wrong imagination

Imagining adverse events, accidents, or scary scenes brings us fear and anxiety, which in turn blurs our judgment and makes us vulnerable to making foolish decisions.

How can we defeat the evil spirit in our minds?

When food goes bad, we don't eat it. Likewise, we feed our minds through what we think. Thus, we should be cautious about the thoughts we allow ourselves to think about. If it is not from God, we should not think about it. If it is difficult to tell, we can ask God. We can ask Christian fellows and read the Bible to know where they are coming from.

We can ignore thoughts we don't want to keep. Just let them go. If there are thoughts that don't go away, pray in the name of Jesus. Reject suggestions from Satan. Thoughts that don't go and stick inside us often have their roots deep within us, so when all attempts do not seem to work, seek Christian counseling, which can help you.

What does the evil spirit do in the emotional sphere?

The evil spirit comes through negative emotions.

In your anger do not sin: Do not let the sun go down while you are still angry, and do not give the devil a foothold.
Ephesians 4:26-27

The evil spirit also stimulates negative emotions. It uses relationships and events to trigger anger, fear, pain, or depression. When we are overwhelmed with negative emotions, it is wise to calm down and control our feelings. Trying too much to find the cause while we are in the middle of having negative emotions leads us to be buried in them. Being buried in emotions is not a way to find the cause of feelings.

God told us to rejoice. What comes from the Holy Spirit is joy and pleasure. When negative emotions come, try to ignore them and try to speak God's words.

Sometimes, some negative feelings don't go away for a long time. It means there is a hole inside us in which we keep falling. In this case, we need inner healing. Pray and ask God for healing.

How do we defeat the evil spirit in the emotional sphere?

> *Humble yourselves, therefore, under God's mighty hand, that he may lift you up in due time. Cast all your anxiety on him because he cares for you. Be alert and of sober mind. Your enemy the devil prowls around like a roaring lion looking for someone to devour. Resist him, standing firm in the faith, because you know that the family of believers throughout the world is undergoing the same kind of sufferings.*
> *1 Peter 5:6-9*

Satan can't manipulate us when we humble ourselves and cast all anxiety on God. Being humble and not being anxious are keys to winning our spiritual battle.

We control our ego by being humble. We can also control anxiety by casting our concerns upon God. Being humble is different from disrespecting ourselves. Jesus showed what it was like to be humble. Meanwhile, the enemy of Christians is not another person, but Satan himself. Thus, Christians should stand not against other people but against Satan, who deceives and manipulates them.

Some people think Satan works in groups, not in individuals. However, Satan's strategy is to destroy each individual and eventually destroy the whole group. Satan looks for a person who can be its channel to destroy an entire community. Anyone spiritually blind can be that channel.

How does the evil spirit work in the verbal sphere?

Ruthless words attack not only people who listen, but also those who speak. Needless criticism and gossiping can harm others. Verbal abuse can remain as deep wounds inside people's hearts. Sometimes it can even last longer and become deeper than the wounds inflicted by a sword.

A troublemaker and a villain, who goes
about with a corrupt mouth.
Proverbs 6:12

Satan uses words to hurt people and trigger negative feelings (Psalms 52:2). People who listen to Satan create perceptions and gossip. They would say,

"We need to pray for him because he is facing these troubles. He is a good leader, but he had this issue…"

We can also be like them, speaking for Satan. Many churches and Christian communities can't be united because of rumors and perceptions.

Talking to oneself also creates negative perceptions.

"I can't do this."

"No one likes me."

"God doesn't care about me."

"Everybody hates me."

"They all want me to go."

These negative thoughts materialize when they are spoken. In fact, God himself created the world by speaking words. As children of God, words that we utter from our mouths also have great power. The way of speaking is a habit. If a person speaks negative things in daily life, that person is used by Satan.

Defeating the evil spirit in the verbal sphere

But if you harbor bitter envy and selfish ambition in your hearts, do not boast about it or deny the truth. Such "wisdom" does not come down from heaven but is earthly, unspiritual, demonic.
James 3:14-15

We should be cautious about what we are going to say. Even if it sounds nice, they become verbal swords that hurt others if they are based on jealousy, judgment, and dispute. So we must always guard ourselves and carefully examine the motives before we speak. Furthermore, we can defeat the evil spirit by speaking out God's word and truth.

"I am a child of God. God protects me. I am worthy because God made me. I have a role in the world. I am filled with God's love, and I can spread this love to others. God blesses my family and neighbors through me. God listens to me."

Speaking out of these words will lead us to win the spiritual battle.

6. Where does our power to win come from?

Children of God have the authority to defeat Satan, as God's spirit is with them. However, it is important to note that it is not their own power that defeats Satan. A police officer stops a truck without using any physical power. It is his authority that stops a truck. Likewise, Christians have authority from God. As it is from God, it always defeats the evil spirit.

> *I have given you authority to trample on snakes and scorpions and to overcome all the power of the enemy; nothing will harm you.*
> *Luke 10:19*

In other words, if Christians don't confront Satan, no one else will. The world is under the control of Satan, so the world alone cannot confront or defeat Satan. Out of all creatures in the world, only Christians are not under the control of the evil spirit. Therefore, only Christians can defeat Satan.

7. How can we use authority and confront the evil spirit?

Confront the evil spirit in the name of Jesus and his precious blood

We can defeat Satan in the name of Jesus. For example, we can say,

"Satan, I rebuke you and command you in the name of Jesus Christ of Nazareth to leave my presence. I bring the blood of Jesus Christ between us. You have no power."

God's words

We can defeat Satan by citing God's words in the Bible. When we speak out the truth found in the Bible, such as God's character and how God loves us, we can defeat the evil spirit in our emotions and minds. We can say,

"God loves me. He didn't do it to punish me. In all things, God works for the good. Go away, Satan. You have no power."

A spiritual man can't defeat the evil spirit for us, and there is no special day to defeat the evil spirit. Whenever we feel the devil's scheme, we should defeat the devil by ourselves. We can do so by putting on the full armor of God, as God himself told us.

The power of the Holy Spirit

We can pray for people possessed by a demon or suffering from a disease with the power of the Holy Spirit. However, to become a person who can reveal the power of the spirit, we should not make the Holy Spirit in us feel sad or disappointed by committing sins.

Speaking out the truth

Victory from spiritual warfare follows when we become more like Jesus Christ in our daily lives. This means that we should focus on God when we speak, when we talk, and when we act throughout our lives. When we live our lives in God's words, we become stronger and more powerful, allowing us to win the spiritual battle.

However, we must also know that just speaking out, "Go away, Satan!" in a loud voice can't defeat the evil spirit if our inner being is still full of sins and lies. At the same time, even if the words were spoken by a little girl, but she had God's words in her mind, then Satan would tremble before her and flee.

CASE

You ended your mother's life

I prayed and prayed, but I felt like I was just speaking to myself. I was seeking God, but I felt distant from God. I did my best in church, but my relationship with people in it wasn't going well. I often got mad and frustrated with people for no reason, which broke my relationships with others. I thought to myself, 'What is wrong with me? Why can't I feel close to God?'

I looked at other people at the BIH seminar. Everyone else was praying in tears. I wanted to feel God just like them. Even if I spoke in tongues and received the Spirit, I still felt distant from God. So I asked God,

"God, what is my problem? Please let me know why I feel distant from you." I was desperate, and a thought popped into my mind:

"Your mother is sick because she got toxemia when she had you."

My family told me a lot about this. My mother suffered from many health issues and even had a kidney transplant. My grandmother and father told me why my mother was sick.

When my mother was pregnant with me, my family was very poor. When she had toxemia during pregnancy, my family told her to have an abortion. However, my mother decided to keep me and continued to work after giving birth to me. Her kidney went bad, and she needed to have a transplant. I have always felt guilty and thought that my mother would have been healthy if she had aborted me.

Whenever my grandmother told me this story, I got upset and screamed at her,

"She should have aborted me! She made things worse!"

I always thought she would be better off if I weren't born. Then, my mother would have been healthy.

But I wasn't sure why this thought came to me when I asked God. I wasn't sure about the relevance between that and my relationship with God. So I decided to have an individual counseling session. During a session, a counselor told me,

"You feel guilty, and that is wrong. Your mother's health issue, kidney transplant, is not either your fault or your mother's. You were born because God wanted you to. It was neither your mother's nor your idea. There were deceptions of demons to oppose God's plan for you, but God has protected you from all threats. You should not feel guilty about your life. It is God who made you. If you genuinely believe in this, you can't say things that disrespect your life. Get confidence in your life from God. Your birth didn't harm your mother. Be confident about your life. "

"So you say it is not my fault?"

"No, it is not your fault."

"All this time... I felt awful and guilty about myself being healthy when my mother was sick."

"Feeling guilty about being healthy is like living your life full of anxiety. You can't stand firm with that negativity."

"You are right. I tried to do more things for my mother because I felt guilty, but I always failed to meet my expectations. I felt inferior and was always angry."

"It's not only you. Anyone who feels guilty can't have a healthy, loving relationship. Guilt makes you feel pressured that you need to do something more for the relationship, but it doesn't work in that way. I guess you feel the same in your relationship with God as with your mother?"

She was right. I did try to do things for God, but it was not from love. So I said, "Yes. I have always felt that my life is a burden that should not have happened. It has never been a good thing. I asked God about my life, but at the same time, I was filled with all this negativity."

"Don't be fooled. God made you and your life. Satan has tried to take your life, but God has protected you. That's why you're here today. Your life is so precious to God."

She was telling the truth. I knew it because it broke the

darkness inside me. All of a sudden, I figured out why I felt distant from God whenever I prayed. I figured out where the guilt that covered my mind came from. I wanted to shout, "I will never be fooled again!"

Now, I have a clear message inside me.

"I didn't make my mother sick. I didn't take her life for my sake. God made me."

Today, I am full of joy and hope. Now, I can stand firm and walk my life with confidence.

CASE

You have a dual personality

A boy wanted to have a one-on-one counseling session during the BIH seminar.

"What do you want to talk about?"

"I am not good at socializing. Especially, I can't say a word to girls."

"Why?"

"Because…I…I have two faces… and I'm afraid that girls would know about it. So I can't talk to them."

He was shaking. There was no confidence in him.

"When did you find out that you have a dual personality?"

"When I was in elementary school."

"How did you know?"

"When I was in fourth grade, my teacher told me so. My friends and I were hanging out during the break. The teacher came into the classroom, so my friends went back to their seats, but I didn't because I didn't see him coming. He told me, "What is wrong with you? I thought you were a Christian. You are a boy with two faces."

"So that's how you found out you have two faces?"

"Yes."

"What do you think Jesus would say if he were there hanging out with you during the break?"

"..."

"Do you think Jesus will call you 'two faces?'"

"I guess he won't... Since then, I have become a different person. I used to have fun at school, but now I am no longer confident about anything..."

We prayed together. God led this boy to the BIH seminar because he wanted to break the most harmful bondage inside him. This bondage took away his confidence and strength, such that he couldn't do anything. Satan used a thoughtless word from a teacher and held a young boy's life.

"Can you share what God would say to you? What did you hear during the prayer?"

"I think he will say, 'It's okay.'"

Tears ran down his face.

CASE

How the curse of Satan shaped my life

I have had so many hurtful experiences in the church. At the same time, I have put most of my time into serving the church. Serving at the church has been my only hope. If someone asked me what my life was like, I would say, "Nothing special."

It's true. There was nothing good about my life. I studied almost every day to teach children at Sunday school. I have always been a winner of Bible trivia competitions at the church. However, I have never felt confident about myself. I always cried every Sunday evening, feeling ashamed of myself. I felt like my students were talking at my back saying, "She knows nothing and has no fun."

The worst thing was watching people say, "God told me…"

I had never heard from God. Regardless of how much time I had put at the church or studied the Bible, I never truly felt God's presence. I felt like God neglected me; that's why I didn't want to go to the Bible study. I hated people at the church. I even disliked my own children because I felt like they only liked their father.

One day, something happened in my life. The wife of our church pastor went to the BIH seminar and started the BIH study group in the church. At first, I didn't even know what BIH was, but it soon changed my life.

In the study group, I was asked about my mother. Every time I talked about my mother, I got upset because I had always believed that my mother hated me.

"Do you really think she hates you?"

The pastor's wife asked me. So I answered, "Yes, I do."

There are many instances proving this belief. For example, when I got married, my mother only gave me a $400 gift but gave a $1000 gift for my brother's wedding. However, the real reason why I hated my mother was that she always told me the thing I hated the most:

"Everyone will disrespect you"

It was from a fortuneteller in my neighborhood. When I was young, I was so sick that I nearly died, and that fortuneteller in my neighborhood told my mother,

"She's going to die. Even if she lives, her life will be disrespected. So it would be better off for her to die now."

Maybe he told her this information just to comfort her and prepare her for the worst scenario.

Since then, my mother would sometimes tell me this story.

"Look, he told me you would die, but you didn't!"

Whenever she told me this story, or whenever it popped into my head, I got so mad.

"Maybe he was right. My life will never be respected. How sad... No one needs me. No one will respect me. It is my destiny."

It was true. The people I trusted betrayed me. I was constantly disrespected. So I believed that what the fortune teller said was true. Then, I blamed God for giving me this kind of life. I hated myself for living this kind of life.

Listening to me talking about all of these things, the pastor's wife told me something that I didn't expect.

"That was a lie. Satan lied."

"What?"

"That was a lie. God makes no one's life like that. No one is destined to have that life. You need to break and defeat the lie right now in the name of Jesus. Let's do it right now."

I was stunned, but what she told me touched my heart. So I prayed with her. When I was praying, the verse John 1:12 popped into my mind. In particular, the word "right" spoke to me.

I thought, 'Yes. I have the right to become a child of God. I thought God had brought me into this world only to be disrespected, but I was wrong. I am a child of God, like others. He gave me the right to be his daughter.'

My heart was filled with God's words, and I believed these words from my heart.

On my way back home, I felt so refreshed and delighted. Everything I saw was beautiful. I thought my life was cursed, but it was no longer true. All this time, I was the most blessed one. I couldn't stop singing praises.

I experienced the living words of God. One verse I read after knowing Satan's lie changed everything. I can't even describe the tremendous changes in my family and marriage. God even blessed my business. One day, my husband told me,

"I also want to know God if he is this good."

I prayed with him, and he received Jesus.

This is a miracle. I used to feel awful about my past, filled with pains and lies. I didn't know how deeply I believed that toxic lie and how hard it kept me and my life, but now my life has changed. My destiny has changed.

SESSION 9

JESUS CAME INTO THE WORLD TO MEET YOU

Jesus came to meet you.

Now, it is your turn to go and meet him.

"Those who seek me will find me."

PURPOSE OF THE SESSION

This session aims to help you know about Jesus, who became human like us. Our inner being is set free from loneliness and bondage when we discover Jesus.

John Squires called the adoption agency, as he was looking for his wife's daughter. John's wife had a daughter when she married her first husband, who died during the Korean War. When her first husband died, she sent her eight-year-old daughter to an orphanage and had lost contact since then. It had been 12 years since she had seen her daughter.

John and his wife were informed that the agency had found her daughter. Her name was Claudia, a singer living in California. Claudia was blind. When Claudia was told that her birth mother was looking for her, she refused to meet her.

"I don't want to see my birth mother. She dumped her blind child. She is not my mother."

Obviously, Claudia held a deep grudge and anger

against her birth mother. However, Claudia's adoptive parents persuaded her to meet her birth mother. So she decided to have a short meeting with her. When Claudia met her birth mother, she was stunned. When her birth mother came to her, called her name, and touched her face, she discovered that her mother was also blind, just like her. As her mother was also blind, she couldn't care for her young child when her husband died in the war.

That's when Claudia found out the truth about why she was sent to an orphanage. She thought she was dumped because she was blind, but she was wrong. When she found out what actually happened, she realized how much her birth mother loved her.

This true story shares similarities with others that depict misunderstandings about God that people often have.

The God of Christianity has a relationship with each of us. Jesus died on the Cross and served as the bridge between God and humans. Anyone who seeks God can be saved and meet him. However, what would happen if we had the wrong idea about God, as Claudia did about her birth mother? We can't have God inside our hearts when we harbor wrong ideas about him.

Jesus didn't want to be a religious god to be worshiped. He wants to have a relationship with us like father and son or loving husband and wife. So he asked God.

that all of them may be one, Father, just as you are in me and I am in you. May they also be in us so that the world may believe that you have sent me.

> *That all of them may be one, Father, just as you are in me and I am in you. May they also be in us so that the world may believe that you have sent me.*
> *John 17:21*

To have a close relationship, as Jesus had wanted, believing in Jesus would not be enough. Instead, all the misunderstandings and grudges inside us should be eliminated so that we can have a relationship with Jesus. We see many Christians who go to church and worship, but whose minds are not with Jesus.

When we keep God only as a religious symbol, emptiness and loneliness stay inside us. Indeed, being religious alone is not a solution to all the hurt we may have been harboring inside us. Loneliness, inferiority, and a sense of being abandoned cannot be solved when we only believe in God as a religion. This kind of superficial belief can't reach our inner being.

What kind of misunderstandings do people have about God? How can they be fixed? How can we have a close relationship with God?

JESUS CAME INTO THE WORLD TO MEET YOU

1. Why does the inner being close its mind to God?

First, we must acknowledge whether we have a misunderstanding of God's role in our lives.

"When I was in trouble, God didn't help me." "God set me to go through all that troubles."

When we have painful memories of when we were young, it is easy to blame God. We may have asked, "Where were you? Why didn't you help me?"

It is impossible to believe his love and kindness when we blame God.

Second, we feel distant from God. "Because he is God, what matters to me is too small for him to take care of."

This idea keeps us away from feeling close to God.

2. What does the Bible say?

You have searched me, Lord, and you know me. You know when I sit and when I rise; you perceive my thoughts from afar. You discern my going out and my lying down; you are familiar with all my ways. For you created my inmost being; you knit me together in my mother's womb.
Psalms 139:13

First, the Bible says that God has always known and protected us, even while we're still in our mother's womb.

Second, the Bible says that Jesus experienced all kinds of pain that humans can ever experience.

He was despised and rejected by mankind, a man of suffering, and familiar with pain. Like one from whom people hide their faces he was despised, and we held him in low esteem.
Isaiah 53:3

3. We become close to God only when we know exactly about Jesus

With the above, we can say that the utmost goal of Satan is to prevent us from knowing the truth about Jesus. One way to distinguish the Holy Spirit from the evil spirit is to check whether it sees Jesus as a human, just like us (John 1 4:1–3).

John the Apostle told us that we should not be deceived

by Satan, as it convinces us to deny that Jesus came into the world in the flesh.

4. The importance of believing that Jesus was a human being just like us

That Jesus was sent to us as a human meant that he was also vulnerable and felt the same pain that we felt as humans. Believing in this truth means we see him just like us—that he lived his life just like us and not as a god who is different from us.

When we find out that Jesus felt the same pain we have, we can experience the power of healing in our lives (John 3:14; 12:32). When we genuinely believe this, we get to believe the power and kindness of Jesus in our lives. We can be brave enough to honestly show our weaknesses and sins before God. We get the power to forgive, and anyone and anything can be forgiven with Jesus. We experience emotional restoration and healing, which lead us to love God and voluntarily follow his words.

5. Jesus is a high priest who brought himself to the sanctuary as the sin offering for our sake

Hebrews 5:1–6 shows two critical conditions to offer sacrifices for one's sins. One is an offering, and the other is a priest who brings an offering to God for humans. Jesus is both an offering and a priest for the sins of the people.

> *For it is declared: "You are a priest forever, in the order of Melchizedek."*
> Hebrews 7:17

Unlike other high priests, Jesus does not need to offer sacrifices day after day. This is because he had already sacrificed for all our sins when he offered himself (Hebrews 7:27).

6. What does the statement "Jesus is a high priest" mean?

In the Old Testament, a high priest offered sacrifices to God for the people. Thus, we can say that Jesus was a high priest and a human who sinned, just like other people. A sin represents homogeneity between a priest and the people. Therefore, a priest also prayed to God for his weakness and acceptance.

Although Jesus lived like a human, just like us, he is not a sinner. Still, he felt the same things we had. Being human is the homogeneity between us and Jesus (Hebrews 5:1–2).

Jesus became a human being.

Jesus became a human, not for angels, but for the sons of Abraham. He prayed for us and our sins as a priest. He felt every pain that we could ever experience. Therefore, he knows our pain. He helps us when we are in pain (Hebrews 2:16–18).

7. People who deny Jesus Christ's humanity

Jesus is God Almighty.

Some people say that Jesus is a god, so he didn't actually feel any pain, hunger, loneliness, and so on, while in human form.

Monophysitism: Jesus is a god. So he is different from a human being.

Some people argue that Jesus only has the character of a god because he is only a god.

Was Jesus human or a god?

The discourse that sees Jesus not as a human being but as a god has resulted in separating Jesus from the people. People who deny Christ's humanity can't have an intimate relationship with him. They can't receive help from Jesus, coming from a relationship with him.

As one person shared, "Jesus is God. He is holy. He is somewhere in the sky. My issues are small shores to him. They are too small for him to care. How dare I discuss my issues with Jesus. He is God. I can't talk to him about pay-ing rent, hair loss, or my selfishness. I feel ashamed talking about these small things with Jesus. So I will not."

The statement "Jesus is God" may sound right, but if we see its outcome (separating Jesus from people) we can tell where the idea came from. It was from the evil spirit.

Denying Christ's humanity results in being afraid of and feeling distant from God.

With fear and distance, people can't go straight to God but pray to Mary and the Saints. Karl Adams describes why people pray to these mediators rather than going straight to Jesus:

"Jesus can't understand everything I went through as a mother. But Mary would, because she was a mother. She had her life as a mother like me. Also, Saint Francis would better understand my situation than God or Jesus because he was also poor, just like me. I feel closer to Mary or Saint Francis than to Jesus. So I will go to Jesus through them."[54]

The Bible says there's only one mediator between God and humans, and that is Jesus Christ. (1 Timothy 2:5). It is clear. Jesus was never ashamed of being our brother. He was fully human in every way (Hebrews 2:17).

---

[54] Adams, Karl. (1959) *Christ our brother*. Collier Books.

8. What was the life of Jesus as a human being?

Birth (Luke 2:7)

Jesus was born in a barn, which was quite uncommon because this place was where farm animals eat and excrete. Christmas cards often have this image of baby Jesus born in a barn covered with beautiful blue lights. However, we all know it is not what a barn actually looks like. No mother wants to give birth to her baby next to animal waste.

This reminds us of a man who came to have a counseling session. He was born in a garbage dump. His life was full of pain and embarrassment because of this memory. Thus, he suffered from a severe inferiority complex.

Jesus's life and his parents' life were neither affluent nor pleasant. It was not like a beautiful fairy tale shown in Christmas cards.

Youth (Luke 2:40; Matthew 6:3)

We know the story of Mary and Jesus through the Bible, written under the guidance of the Holy Spirit. When Jesus started his ministry, people in his neighborhood didn't listen to him and just called him "Mary's boy." Jesus was never called the "son of Joseph." Instead, Jesus was the son of Mary, the unmarried woman who was considered impure.

At that time, Jesus was just a boy with an embarrassing family background. His mother had him outside of the marriage. His father was a poor carpenter. Sometimes, people in Jesus's neighborhood thought his family was insane.

Being tested (Matthew 4:1–11)

The devil always uses the top three things that people seek the most. The devil tempted Jesus with wealth, fame, and power. In most cases, people betray God to have these three things in their lives. When the devil used these to tempt Jesus, it showed that Jesus was also human, just like us.

Jesus didn't use a magic stick, tricks, or any power to conjure whatever he wanted. Jesus never passed a crisis in his life with his mighty power. Even when he was killed, he suffered all kinds of pain.

The first human, Adam, disobeyed God for his desire. However, Jesus obeyed every word of God and laid down every will and need while he was a human.

9. Isaiah was moved by God and prophesized a Messiah, Jesus Christ, whom God will send (Isaiah 53)

He is soft, like a seed leaf

A seed leaf is so soft that even a baby can cut it. Jesus came into the world without any armor or weapon, so anyone could persecute him. He lived his life, not as a strong man. He was a vulnerable man, much like a seed leaf.

Drought: Wilderness where you can't find any help

Plants growing on dry land are weak and vulnerable. Many people came from a family, much like a dry land without any nutrition and moisture. These people lived their lives all by themselves. They worked when their friends were playing. They made money for their family, while their friends had so many nice gifts from their parents.

Jesus is the king of all kings. However, he didn't have anything when he was a human being. He didn't know anyone famous or had any family to support him. No one was behind Jesus. He was completely alone when he was in the utmost pain. He was by himself when he was on the Cross. No one fully understood him. Jesus was from a place that no one in this world knew about. He didn't have any blood relationships. He had to stand by himself on "dry land." Yet no one in this world is alone like Jesus.

Being neglected

Jesus was not a good-looking man. He was neither tall nor physically fit. People neglected and disrespected Jesus. The miracles he made were neglected. However, the Bible says that we can have peace and can be considered worthy of everything because Jesus was despised. Jesus considered despicable people his friend and apostles, and we are also one of them.

Illness

Jesus's face was so disfigured beyond that of any human being (Isaiah 52:14).

People treated Jesus as a worm, not a man (Psalms 22:6).

People despised and rejected Jesus like one from whom people hide their faces (Isaiah 53:3; Leviticus 13:45).

The appearance of Jesus was very different from what we saw in films or paintings.

10. Why did Jesus choose to live a life full of pain?

The devil tempted Jesus to save himself from the Cross using his almighty power. The apostles also wanted Jesus to save himself from the Cross.

However, Jesus chose to die on the Cross, powerless. According to the Bible, Jesus died on the Cross as a human being so that he can be a "top priest" who can atone for people's sins (Hebrews 2:17–18).

Jesus chose to be a friend who can share pains and sorrows rather than a god who is worshiped. Furthermore, he served as a sin offering for our sins when he became a human being. Jesus never used his almighty power. Instead, he obeyed God's words until his death. Therefore, anyone who receives Jesus can be born again and have the power to live a life like Jesus.

Jesus suffered from all kinds of pains, just like us. People dying in the wilderness were healed when they saw Moses's bronze snake. Likewise, when we find that Jesus experienced the exact same pain as ours, such pain is healed immediately. Our fears become our courage. This is a miracle we all can have, and only those who have experienced it can validate this truth.

If there's pain in your life and you realize that Jesus also had the same pain in his life, you sort of have "eye contact" with Jesus on the Cross. This is a shelter where wounded people can be protected and healed. This is why the devil keeps telling lies, deceiving us into thinking that Jesus is a god and not a human being.

When people suffering from betrayal realize that Jesus also experienced the same thing, as shown in the Bible, the pain is transformed into a kind of power that helps us understand how Jesus felt in the face of betrayal.

When people who can't forgive find out how they attacked and hurt Jesus in the Bible, they also acquire the power to forgive. Furthermore, people can also say that they can accept the pain and hurt as Jesus did.

As we become close friends with Jesus, the relationship becomes deeper as we get to know more and more about his life as a human being. We become his friend as we come to know all his suffering and pain as a human being.

In this way, we can live our lives with God.

This is the life that Jesus wanted us to have. He prayed for us to have this relationship before he died on the Cross.

CASE

I also suffered from poverty, just like your father

I studied theology. However, no matter how I tried to be a good Christian and receive the Holy Spirit, a fear inside me didn't disappear. I was afraid of people. I had a fear of public speaking. I always felt like I did something wrong. I didn't know why, but I had this guilt and fear all the time.

I expected God would want me to do something in my life. So I went to study theology. However, fear and guilt only grew deep inside me. I was afraid of God and felt distant from him.

I came to the BIH seminar, which allowed me to have a different perspective. I realized that I should ask God why I felt guilty rather than condemn myself all the time. I asked God, and he immediately showed me a scene. I felt like he was waiting for me to ask him!

I saw a scene from my childhood. My family was very poor. One day, I was hanging out with my friends at home, and I saw my father coming. He looked like a homeless person. I felt ashamed of him. So I told my friend,

"He is not my father."

God reminded me of this moment, and I soon realized the cause of the fear and guilt that had followed me throughout my life. I asked God for forgiveness for denying and feeling ashamed of my father. Satan used this memory to make me feel guilty. So I prayed. However, I didn't feel better. Instead, I asked myself, "Why were we so poor?"

I realized that I was mad at God.

"My father wouldn't be like that if we were not poor."

I was very emotional and upset. Moreover, I felt disappointed.

"I came to the BIH seminar, and I still have unfinished work with God. What should I do?"

It was in the last session of the seminar that God resolved my unfinished sorrow. The session was about Jesus coming into the world as a human being. During the session, I heard Jesus talking to me:

"I was poor, just like your father. I didn't have any good clothes to wear, just like your father."

When I heard the voice, all the grudges inside me toward God collapsed.

I thought to myself, 'So I wasn't the only one who had a poor life. God and his son were also poor like me.'

Since then, I haven't felt any more grudges. I am no longer ashamed of my childhood and family.

I don't feel any more fear.

I left a theological school because I no longer needed to study theology to believe in God. Instead, I went to school to study what I wanted to study.

I love God more than I've ever loved.

CASE

They also called me demon-possessed

She was a housewife and mother of two children. Everything changed when she received the Holy Spirit.

When she received the Spirit and spoke in tongues, everyone was stunned. She spoke swear words in English when she was speaking in tongues. People in her church told her that she was demon-possessed, so they introduced her to a Christian exorcist. She moved in with the exorcist for a month. While she was there, we learned that physical violence was always involved whenever she prayed with the exorcist. The exorcist said that she was possessed by the ghosts of soldiers, so she was treated as a ghost, not as a human. The exorcist also didn't allow her to speak and forced her to spit all the time, telling her there was also an evil spirit in her spit.

Unfortunately, her condition worsened, so she was sent to a mental institution. When she came back home, she couldn't sleep with her children. She was afraid that her children might also be possessed by the evil spirit in her. She believed that an evil spirit resided in her spit, so she didn't share anything with her children. She didn't let her children touch or eat the foods she ate.

She was told that she was having a nervous breakdown. A doctor said it couldn't be cured. It was not only her but also her family who suffered severely during all this time.

When I met her, she was in pain and said she indeed felt there was an evil spirit inside her. She was suffering from insomnia and heart disease. She had not been living the life of a human for the past ten years.

However, I disagreed with her notion that she was possessed because I sensed her warm gesture and kindness. People possessed by the evil spirit for so long can't have such warmth. So every time I met her, I told her,

"You are not possessed."

She also wanted to believe that. However, she couldn't. Whenever she felt something inside her, she was certain she was possessed. For the past ten years, her mind was filled with the idea that she was demon-possessed.

It was essential to take time to look into her life for healing. So I met her regularly. We looked into every past event of her life. By looking into her past, we found out why she cursed when she prayed in tongues.

Her father served in the US military in South Korea. When her parents fought with each other, her father cursed in English. She heard this when her mother was pregnant with her. It remained deep inside her subconscious and came out when she prayed through the Spirit. As we had more sessions, she showed several changes. First, she started to feel angry.

"I feel like I am someone else. Most of all, I get mad at people. I wasn't like this. Whenever I get mad or feel anger, I try to avoid it, because I think those emotions are from the evil spirit inside me. So people thought I was nice to all. But I wasn't. I was hiding my anger. So I felt terrible inside. But now, I am not afraid of feeling angry. When people make me upset, I allow myself to be mad at them, and I feel like I'm normal."

However, as she started to feel emotions, she faced a hurdle. She couldn't control her rage toward other people who destroyed her life - the ones who thought she was demon-possessed. She was furious and felt so much pain.

I said, "You need to forgive them to be free from the pain."

She cried and screamed.

"How? How can I forgive them? No one had been through the things I had. Jesus had so much pain in his life, but even he didn't have what I had. People treated me like a monster. I have lived in fear of demon possession for the past ten years. I couldn't even take care of my children. Jesus doesn't know the pains I have. No one in this world knows."

I was speechless. I didn't know what to say to move

her mind, but then God spoke to me,

"I heard that too. They also called me demon-possessed."

I suddenly remember a scene where spiritual leaders called Jesus demon-possessed in front of the public. I told her what God said.

When she heard about it, the grudges and anger that filled her suddenly faded. She cried and cried. She told me,

"Jesus had the same thing. If Jesus forgave them, I would forgive them too."

I saw all the pain that covered her move to Jesus. This spoke to me clearly about why Jesus came to us. I realized,

'Yes... This is why Jesus came to us. He came to heal our sorrow. He came to set us free. This is it. He entered into suffering so that we could share our pains with him. We can connect with Jesus because he suffered from things we suffered. This is how he heals us. This is how we can be healed through Jesus!'

I witnessed how Jesus comforts our pain and how powerful it is. Its strength comes from the fact that Jesus also felt the same kind of pain we have.

CASE

The story of a teacher

I was ironing clothes when I felt a sudden surge of anger directed at someone. The event that I recalled happened more than decades ago, and it still makes me mad whenever I think about it.

I recently graduated from college, and it was my first year as a teacher. There was a colleague who was older than me. I was new to everything, so I depended on him. However, he was always mad at me and pointed out things that I did wrong. He even said to me,

"I think you shouldn't be a teacher. Working at the same school with you ruins my reputation."

I didn't know why, but I was always afraid of him. I didn't say a word or make an excuse for myself. Working with him was a nightmare. I just kept thinking,

'It's in the past. I am now married to a pastor. I shouldn't get mad...'

However, I was also upset at myself, who just couldn't let it go. To be honest, it was not the worst thing that happened in my life, but why did I hate him the most? Whenever I remember him, I couldn't pray and became emotionally overwhelmed.

One day, I thought about him again, and it made me feel terrible. I wanted to be free from it. I wanted to let it go. So I prayed to God, but then I also got mad at God.

"God, I think I can't forgive him. I hated him so much whenever I tried to forgive him. God, where were you when he was bullying me?"

Then God allowed me to "see" a scene. My colleague was saying mean things to me, and I was standing there. However, I saw that Jesus was also there, standing next to me. He was looking down and saying nothing, just like me. When I saw Jesus next to me, I felt the anger go away. That's how I forgave him.

I can't forget the look Jesus had while he was standing next to me. It was the most powerless look of Jesus I had ever seen. Yet at the same time, it was also the most powerful force that changed me.

SESSION 10

FROM HEALING TO GROWTH

Inner healing through the Holy Spirit is just like having surgery, which means recovery also takes time. Sufficient time and nutrition are needed for a patient to recover after surgery. Likewise, inner healing requires continued care.

A heavy rock that has hurt you has been removed. Now, your heart is like rich soil, ready to receive a seed leaf.

PURPOSE OF THE SESSION

This session discusses your role after receiving inner healing from the Holy Spirit. Your cooperation is needed to ensure that such inner healing will help your inner being grow. Depending on your willingness to cooperate with the Holy Spirit, the seed inside you will grow faster or slower. Thus, your role is crucial in its development.

You have the power to make inner healing grow your inner being. It will be the new routine of your life.

When all our enemies heard about this, all the surrounding nations were afraid and lost their self-confidence, because they realized that this work had been done with the help of our God.

> *When all our enemies heard about this, all the surrounding nations were afraid and lost their self-confidence, because they realized that this work had been done with the help of our God.*
> *Nehemiah 6:16*

"Am I really ready for a change?"

"Isn't inner healing a one-time emotional experience?"

"What if my past and old habits come back?"

People raise these questions. They had spiritual experiences and became spiritually emotional. However, a few months later, these spiritual emotions disappear, and it makes them think,

"It doesn't work."

When Nehemiah tried to rebuild the wall, people laughed at him. However, he was eventually able to rebuild the wall in 50 days. Later on, the people who laughed at him became afraid of him. You must know that the thoughts raised inside you that make you doubt your inner healing and the changes in you are not from God, but from the evil spirit.

The children of God who received the spirit of Jesus should have renewed minds. However, it takes time, like the building of a new wall. Most cases shared in this book were testimonies from the BIH seminar. People who shared these testimonies are all still in the process of inner healing. Given that the experience of inner healing from the BIH seminar is not the final stage but just the start of the process, their healing hasn't been completed yet.

The evil spirit, however, may still implant the wrong ideas into our minds,

"Everything should be completed by now; if not, they are all fake. If it is real, you should have spiritual feelings. If you feel nothing, it means that they were all fake and one-time emotional experiences."

This is a lie, and we should not listen to lies. God led Nehemiah to rebuild the wall that had collapsed for seven decades. God will do the same in you. God will rebuild and renew your mind and your whole being.

God will cleanse you, and you will be clean. He will give you a new heart and put a new spirit in you. He will remove the old stone in you so that you can follow his decrees and be mindful of keeping his words (Ezekiel 36:25-27). The blood of Christ guarantees this promise of God. He will cleanse your body and mind just like he cleansed your spirit (Hebrews 9:13-14). However, while God is doing his job, you need to do your part.

For the past three decades, we have witnessed changes in the lives of people who have joined the BIH seminar. These changes started with the seminar and continued to impact their lives and relationships. We have witnessed so many cases where people experienced the healing of illnesses within their bodies. The wave started by the Holy Spirit is expected to last for a long time.

Then, what is our role?

FROM HEALING TO GROWTH

1. Keep renewing our minds

We already discussed the importance of the mind in Sessions 2 and 8. Here, we would like to elaborate on the paths of our minds.

Your life is a sculpture that your mindset has shaped. Our minds are hidden, but they come out and shape our lives. Our mindset determines how we behave. Our behaviors turn into habits that eventually shape our lives. Therefore, if our mindset stays in the past, we will stay in the past, regardless of the spiritual healings we experience. However, if we acquire a new mindset and way of thinking, healing continues in our lives and will change our personalities and entire lives forever.

A route from A to B doesn't pop up suddenly; rather,

it represents an accumulation of the same choices. It becomes the route when we continuously take a particular route from A to B. There is a route inside us that we are familiar with. It is inside us because we always took that route. It is not easy to take other routes unless there is an earthquake on that route that we can't pass. This is what we need to do. We need to change the route we used to take and build a new route. The Holy Spirit takes control of building a new route. Our role is to be glad about having a new route.

In line with the above, there are specific routes in our mindset that must be eliminated.

We have routes in our mindset that refer to our ways of thinking.

Our way of thinking from the past doesn't go away just because we become Christians. Our old way of thinking still occupies a significant part of us.

The way of thinking we have from the past blocks the way of God inside our minds.

God gave Canaan to the Israelites. While the Canaanites were living in Canaan, they became strong and tried to kill the Israelites to keep Canaan.

Canaan was God's land. However, those who occupied the land argued for their ownership of the land. Likewise, the old way of thinking in our mindset is in conflict with their ownership of our minds. They combine all kinds of knowledge that are mostly against God's words. That is why there are battles inside us.

God told us to "Kill every Canaanite."

Likewise, God said to kill every old way of thinking in our minds because it will damage us again and block the Holy Spirit's entry inside us. Therefore, we need to take over Canaan to end our wandering and see the blessing of God. God told Israelites to kill everyone in Canaan, including children. Why? It was the children in Canaan who later destroyed Israel. Likewise, there is an old way of thinking that seems innocent, just like that of children. They have innocent labels, such as "culture" or "tradition." With these innocent labels, they don't seem like a threat or evil. However, they are used as a tool to encourage us to rebel against God's words and lead our minds to despair.

The way of thinking that has been instilled inside us for a long time strongly holds our inner being.

It is like a strong glue or sticky resin. It is from the evil spirit that is trying to deceive us. Unfortunately, people don't even know that they are stuck with that resin.

A man suffered from his old way of thinking, which held him hostage for his entire life. He was sick and got into an accident all the time. He had surgeries over and over again and had been in so many accidents. So he volunteered to go to a remote area in a foreign country as a missionary because he thought he would die anyway soon. Later on, he decided to come to the BIH seminar, in which God told him about the inner thoughts that had held him.

When he was young, a teacher from his Sunday school told him that they needed to bring their parents to church because, otherwise, his family would be cursed for three generations. As his parents were not Christians, he thought he and his children would be cursed. This thought was planted in his mind and eventually grew into a persistent idea. Hence, living with such a thought, he had a life of illnesses and accidents.

He didn't question his teacher's words. He just believed it. He just waited for the curse to be over. When his children underwent surgery, he just thought it was because of the curse in his family. Satan used this thought in him. It brought continued accidents and diseases to his family. Unfortunately, he just accepted them.

During the seminar, he realized that it was Satan's lie. So he prayed to defeat the lie that had held his life. Since then, he has been free from the thought of a generational curse. A few years later, I met him again, and he told me that his family haven't had any accidents or diseases since then.

His story is proof that our mindset doesn't stay inside us. It comes out as our lives.

How can we build a new way of thinking?

Distinguish what comes from God from those that do not come from him.

If there is a thought from the evil spirit, and we think this is from God or ourselves, we can't defeat them. If we don't have the strong will to defeat them, the Holy Spirit can't help us. Therefore, it is crucial to know exactly where such a thought is coming from. How can we tell whether it is from God or not?

1) Examine a thought not by yourself but through conversation

Good Christian counseling helps us examine our thoughts. However, it is not easy to have counseling all the time. So Jesus sent us the Holy Spirit as a counselor and helper. Christians can ask the Holy Spirit to help them distinguish whether a particular thought is from God.

The conversation consists of two steps: speaking and listening. No matter how long and hard you pray, it is not a conversation if you don't listen to what God says. If you don't listen, you can't tell whether a thought is from God, and you can't change your way of thinking. The following figure shows what happens when we don't listen to God. When we don't listen or don't ask God, there is only a vicious cycle that leads us to despair.

Figure 6

This is an example of a path or a way of thinking. It is a fixed vicious cycle that leads to despair.

2) Use the Bible as a standard

Use words from the Bible as a standard to distinguish the origin of your thoughts. If the thought is not in accordance with what the Bible says, it is not from God. Even if it is accepted in society, the Bible should be the standard, not the society or opinion of the majority.

For example, today, many people have sex without love. People have sex outside of marriage. However, the Bible doesn't allow people to have sexual relationships outside of marriage. Which idea should we follow?

The Bible hasn't changed over time because it is not ethics but the only truth that shows how we should live. We should have the Bible as the plumb line of our thoughts.

3) See the outcome of your thoughts

Does this thought lead you to have courage and love for God and other people? Or does it make you feel unstable, nervous, and depressed? We can tell the origin of the thought by its outcome.

Figure 7

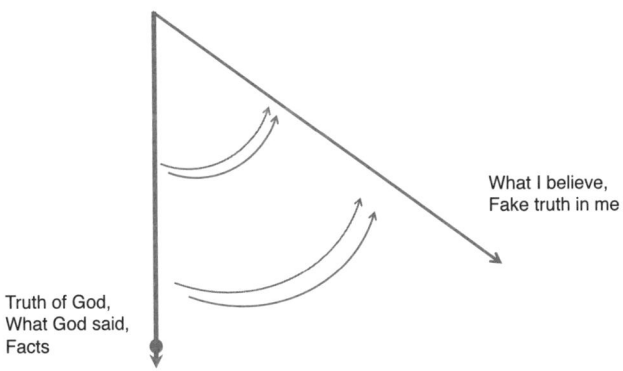

Each arrow shows the thoughts inside us. The arrow on the left shows the truth from God that doesn't change. The arrow on the right represents our changing standards. Our thoughts are based on one of these two arrows. If our thoughts are based on the arrow on the right, as it is moving, it leads to an unstable life. We can't have stability with standards that change depending on circumstances, culture, time, etc.

4) Break the old and build a new way of thinking

The following figure shows an example of the old way of thinking.

Figure 8 Ways of thinking

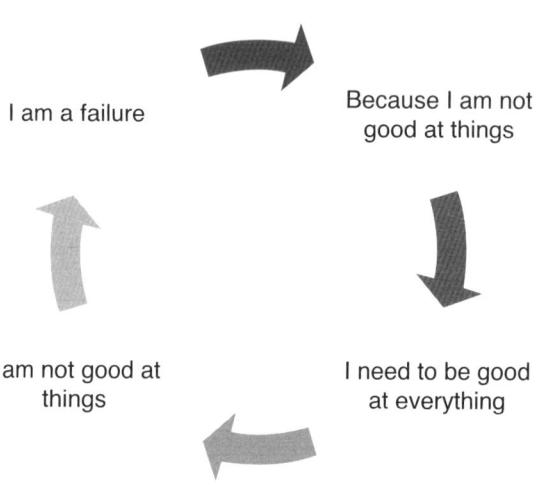

The following prayer can be used to break the old way of thinking that leads to negativity in our lives:

"I pray in the name of Jesus Christ. The idea that I need to be good at everything to not be a failure is not the idea of God. I will not accept this idea again."

We can defeat all thoughts that are not from God through prayer. Our minds are filled with false wisdom, cultures, traditions, or wrong messages from society that are against God's words. We should be cautious and look into each perception and belief that we have. It is like a cleaning process. Go through your mind and find ideas that are not from God. Defeat those ideas and, in their place, fill your mind with thoughts from God. It will bring huge joy to your life. This is how to build a new way of thinking.

There's no way that something can be too old to be fixed. Anything old should be replaced with a new way of thinking. The old way of thinking that is not from God leads to death. Furthermore, it impacts not only ourselves but also our family and our children.

When we try to hold the thoughts from God, the Holy Spirit helps us. What we need to do is try to hold the thoughts of God.

Choosing to keep thoughts that are not from God is a form of disbelief, which is the original sin of humans. Disbelief is not about belief; it is determined by choosing ideas and thoughts that are not from God. Indeed, disbelief leads people to death.

God told Adam and Eve the truth. However, the evil spirit told them other thoughts.

"God lied to you. You will not die but will be better off if you eat this fruit."

When there's a battle inside us in which two conflicting thoughts try to dominate us, depending on the choice we make, we may have a different life. No one can avoid the consequences of their choices. We all live once and will be judged in the end (Hebrews 9:27).

Inner healing in God always brings changes to the mind, and our emotions are the outcomes of our mind. Therefore, the right way of thinking leads to the right emotions. If there are no changes in our minds, healing won't last regardless of how spiritual or emotional we may feel.

2. Try to express how you really feel before God

We should be honest about our feelings before God. It is not about being mad and hostile to God; it is about expressing our pains and sorrows to him. In particular, try not to judge your emotions based on religious or ethical standards. Like describing the symptoms we have to a doctor, we must tell God everything that we feel without holding back.

Some people feel guilty about having anger, so they don't tell God about the anger inside them or find someone else to blame. In this case, the wounds inside them cannot be healed. Regardless of how ugly they are, we should be honest about all of our feelings and ask God for help. In this way, the Holy Spirit will heal and cleanse us.

3. Try not to be too analytic

Some people become too analytic. Why?

- They haven't personally experienced healing from

the Holy Spirit. They read inner healing books and refer to other people's inner healing experiences, leading them to take over the role of the Holy Spirit. This is analysis, not healing.
- When people only focus on being stable and in a good mood, there can't be healing, but just analysis.
- When people only focus on being righteous rather than having a proper relationship with Jesus, again, there can't be healing, but just analysis.

When people continue only to be consoled and not repent for the sins they committed, the healing process stops.

The crucial goal of healing is to renew one's relationship with God. However, if people focus only on their minds, not God, then they may experience the following side effects:

- It keeps us inside ourselves. Exploring what's inside us and staying inside us are different. The former leads to improvement, while the latter leads to psychological issues, critical attitudes, and arrogance. Of course, there will be no changes in our lives. It leads us to have a doubt about the healing that we can receive from the Holy Spirit.
- Some feel like they know everything about their minds and the causes of every issue. However, they don't see any changes in their emotions nor in their relationships with others.

- The healing inside them can't lead them to grow, and such growth won't be sustained.

Therefore, it is crucial not to be too analytic during the inner healing procedure.

4. Express your love and interest in other people

Doing volunteer work or participating in outreach projects balances our outward and inward energy. Loving others keeps our focus on God, not on ourselves. A small act of love without intent empowers our inner being.

Furthermore, volunteer work helps us understand the truth. We always get a better understanding of the truth when we follow them. When we care for others, we can guard ourselves from deceptions that can encourage us to be too analytic.

5. Go to a church and Christian community where you can share your weakness and vulnerability.

People who follow the Holy Spirit empower their church and care for neighboring churches. The church is a healing community in which every weakness and issue by the evil spirit is renewed and healed through the relationships we forge there and the worship and prayers that we perform.

However, don't be disappointed because you can't find a church or Christian community where you can be healed.

A small group of yours can be the ideal place for you. Pray to have the power to form your own group as a place where people can share in God. Everything starts with one person. You can be that person.

6. Be active in reading the Bible and learning it by heart

Be confident that you can find answers from the Bible. The Bible has every wisdom and all the answers needed by humans. In fact, it has answers that no other psychological literature has. When you have questions about your mind, spirit, and feelings, read the Bible, and ask God for the right answer. The Holy Spirit will guide you to find it.

7. Take your time

The growth of one's inner being takes time—much more than you may have expected. However, be steadfast. Don't give up. The Holy Spirit will continue his work, and your cooperation is essential. Meanwhile, read the book of Nehemiah.

Rebuilding our minds is more complex than rebuilding Nehemiah's collapsed wall. While challenging and complex, the Holy Spirit will complete the job. We should be patient in rebuilding and renewing our minds so that no one can damage and break them.

Healing and Restoration in families

While it may take many years to see significant healing and restoration inside a family, inner healing in God always brings restoration inside a family.

The highlight of Biblical Inner Healing ministry is seeing all family members—the father, mother, daughters, and sons—praising God.

CASE

It is too heavy to carry

The story of the husband

I was born into a Christian family. I became a missionary when I was in college. Since then, I have worked on campus, preaching to college students. I met my wife at the missionary organization. It seemed beautiful to have a ministry with a wife. For all these years, we have done our best together. However, during the missionary conference this year, I wanted to quit everything.

"Jesus Christ! Gospel of Jesus to the world!"

At first, it was nice. So I decided to sacrifice my life for it. However, this year, I started to feel like I don't have any more energy to continue. I couldn't pray. I only said,

"God, I want to die. Please take me. I have too much weight on my shoulders."

I had a beautiful wife and children, but that didn't make me feel better. I was so tired of my life full of ministries and works. But then, I heard this voice inside me.

"No. You can't die."

So I asked back, "Then what should I do?"

"It's mine to carry. I will carry them for you."

Come to me, all you who are weary and burdened, and I will give you rest. Take my yoke upon you and learn from me, for I am gentle and humble in heart, and you will find rest for your souls. For my yoke is easy and my burden is light.
Matthew 11:28-30

With God's words, my whole life flashed before my eyes. I suddenly understood why God told me this.

A few months ago, I went to the BIH seminar. The lecturer said,

"In this seminar, God wants to take off your worn cloth and wash you."

It spoke to me. I thought God was telling me something. I always felt like a beggar, having dirt on my face and clothes. So I had a habit of rubbing my face when talking to others. So when I heard God's word during the seminar, I thought God wanted to do something to me, but nothing happened. Since then, some years have passed.

Today, God told me that he would carry my baggage. I knew why he told me that. He really knew me. When my life flashed before my eyes, with God's voice, I started to understand the things that happened in my life.

My family was unhappy when I was young because of my father's adultery. One day, when I went to the church, the ladies talking to my mother told me,

"Sangho, never be like your father. We feel terrible for your mother."

I felt embarrassed. It made me feel like I was not clean. I started to believe that I was like my father, an unclean person.

So since then, whenever I talk to people, I have had the habit of touching my face to remove the invisible dirt on my face. I tried to be confident and keep my voice loud. I worked hard in church. I have done many things to prove that I am not dirty.

I was in elementary school when I found out that my father cheated on my mother. I looked for someone to talk to. My mother was praying by herself. None of my sister or brother wanted to talk with me. We all suffered. I didn't have anyone, so I wanted to die. I carried a rope in my bag.

However, at the same time, I felt responsible that I somehow needed to take care of my family. When I got married, I wanted to rely on my wife. However, I didn't get consolation from my family or my wife. For me, my home was not a place to rest. It was another baggage that I needed to carry. This was worsened by the many works that I needed to do for God. I felt like I no longer had the energy to carry them. So I asked God to kill me, just like when I was young.

However, God showed me the scene when I was young and told me that they were not mine to carry. I didn't know I had carried this much weight on my shoulder. I didn't know why I felt so tired, but now I know.

"God, please take my baggage. Please carry them for me."

When I said this to God, I felt so relieved.

"God, I feel so relieved. I now have the energy to live."

At the same time, I thought about my wife. I realized that I had handed over the heavy baggage to my wife. I prayed in tears for forgiveness.

"God forgive me. You sent my wife to love, but I have only given her my burdens."

I came home and told my wife what had happened. She understood me. Since then, I have seen changes in my family and ministry.

God carries my burdens. I am now fully confident in myself and not afraid to show who I am. I can give love to the people I meet.

The story of the wife

When I met my husband, he was a strong man with integrity. Recently, I was shocked when I learned that he had pretended all along and tried to hide his inferiority.

When I got married, I was disappointed in him. I started

to disrespect him. I thought we were mature Christians. However, our marriage met several troubles that I didn't expect. So my marriage gave me huge disappointment in my husband and in myself. I guess my husband may have felt the same.

We had a chance to come to the BIH seminar twice, and each of us found who we were in God. It gave us an answer to solve the many issues in our relationship.

When my husband went to the BIH seminar for the first time, he prayed and wanted to find out why he felt dirty. At the same time, I was praying by myself and saw a scene where Jesus washes my husband and brings him to me with new clothes.

During the seminar, my husband didn't find out why he felt dirty at first, but I was sure that God continued his healing work on my husband. My husband became exhausted. This was when we came to the BIH seminar for the second time.

During the second BIH seminar, my husband shared his honest feelings with God. He always did his best for God and told him he wanted to die. It was the time when God told him why he felt so tired.

My husband asked me to forgive him. I was listening to him, and I started to understand the things he had done. My husband got upset when he saw me praying in tears. I didn't understand why it upset him, but now I do. It reminded him of his mother, praying in tears when she found out her husband cheated on her.

Now, I feel that my husband accepts and respects me. I feel comfortable being with my husband. I see tremendous changes in him. Before, he was always impatient and nervous. Now, he seems relieved and relaxed. Back then, whenever we argued, he couldn't control his temper, but now, he is relaxed, calm, and ready to listen to me even when we disagree.

Watching changes in my husband also brought me changes. I became generous to him and wanted to do something nice for him. We had a lot of disagreements before, and it took me so much energy to listen to his words, but now I listen to him and yield. It is not that difficult now. We still argue sometimes, but this is different from our previous arguments. I also see changes in my son. He laughs more. We are a happy family now.

CASE

A knife in my hand

The story of Hyekyung's mother

No one knows what I am really like. When I met people, I barely talked. When I was in church, I was nice to all, but at home, I was always upset and said brutal things to my husband and children. I always took my anger out on them. I didn't even try to control my temper.

I was always upset, nervous, and anxious. There was no reason to be, but I always woke up in anxiety. I went to church to relieve this unpleasant emotion, but it didn't go away. I knew there was something wrong with me.

I had the chance to attend the BIH seminar and a subsequent counseling session. At first, I found it very difficult to express my anxiety. The counselor asked me to share the most painful memories I'd ever had.

As soon as she asked me, I recalled one incident. It was something I did to my daughter.

"One day, I was about to stab my daughter."

"What exactly did you do?"

"She was three years old and didn't listen to me. So I grabbed her and brought her to the basement. I showed her a kitchen knife and threatened to kill her if she didn't listen to me. I remember that she didn't say she was sorry."

I was embarrassed and felt pain about what I had done to her.

"Did you learn it from someone?"

"I did, from my mother."

I was surprised at myself. It just came out, and I felt immense sorrow inside me. I couldn't stop crying.

The counselor told me what God said to her,

"You have thrown out the knife."

As soon as I heard the words, the left side of my heart became so light that I felt like I could fly. I felt something heavy calming down my heart as it trembled from anxiety.

Then, I recalled that my mother always threatened me with a knife whenever I threw a tantrum. I realized that I was doing the same thing to my daughter. I felt devastated. I was doing to my children the very act that I hated the most. Yet God forgave me. He let me throw out the knife I had been holding onto for years.

On my way home, I can't stop praising God.

'The power of God that set me free from the sin...I saw it. It was why I felt so nervous and insecure. I was doing the same to my children. God knew everything…'

I started to feel scared of God that he knows it all and watches everything I do. It became the turning point in my life and particularly helped me overcome my depression.

I haven't been my mother's favorite child. She always gave more to my brother than to me. So it was hard to love myself. My husband is a good man, but I don't know how to receive his love. I had always thought that he was going to break my heart. I blamed him for everything. I always told him how he made me disappointed.

Moreover, my mother has never given me love. I have never felt warmth from her. I think that was why I always felt disappointed and sad. But God told me exactly who I am.

"You are from God."

It broke something about me that I had for the past 53 years. I didn't know who I was. I felt insecure and thought I was useless. I am so grateful to God for telling me the truth.

Since then, when I see people treat their children carelessly on the streets, I feel sad and want to tell them to stop.

"Please don't treat your child like that. Be a good parent. Don't make the same mistake as I did."

I have cried so much since the BIH seminar. I cried because I felt so sorry for my children. I cried because I felt so grateful to God. I cried because I felt so sad for people who were still in pain like I was. There are so many people out there who suffer from painful memories. I went to fortunetellers, cults, and psychiatrists, but all of them couldn't fix the pain. I want to tell people that God's love is the only way to heal the pain.

I shared my healing experience with my children, relatives, and neighbors. I emphasized how important it was to have inner healing in God. My family members and neighbors were convinced to go to the BIH seminar. Now, I see restoration in their families and lives as well.

One particular thing I am grateful for is how God healed all the pain that I gave to my daughter. It has been four years since God removed a knife from my hand. Recently, God completed the process by also healing my daughter.

My children always called me a mean mom. They only liked their father because of how I treated them and my husband. I understood that, but I felt lonely. However, God let my daughter understand why her mother had so much anger. When my daughter told me about what God told her and that she understood me, all my grudges were gone. When my husband heard my daughter saying what she knew, he apologized to me as well, saying,

"Please forgive me. You were such a nice woman, but I made you cry and live in pain for the past years."

When I heard my husband, I apologized to him too. It was me who should be forgiven. We hugged each other and cried. We used to be in a long, dark tunnel, but now, I feel like we are finally emerging from this tunnel. Our relationship has been renewed, like we are on our honeymoon.

The story of the daughter, Hyekyung

One day, my mother went to a Christian seminar and asked me to forgive her. She told me something about the basement. She kept crying and asking me to forgive her. It was unexpected, and I remember that I felt awkward.

Watching her crying, I was skeptical and wondered whether it would last, because it was not the first time this had happened. Sometimes, my mother would get so upset and then suddenly become nice to us. So I thought this was just another temporary change.

My mother kept asking me to forgive her, so I just said yes, even if I didn't know what to forgive. She kept telling me about the BIH seminar, and I hated it. I didn't get why the BIH seminar was the only way to be healed.

Since then, I waited for my mother to be mad at me as she did before. Whenever I saw her being mad at us, I was like, "I knew it. It wasn't a real thing."

However, I began to notice a slight change in her. I noticed that she cried a lot more than she did. I was once washing dishes and broke a plate. I got nervous and waited for my mother to scream at me. However, she didn't get mad at me, but worried about my hand instead. These small changes in my mother made me curious about what really happened at the BIH seminar.

So I decided to come to the seminar. My brother, aunt, and cousins also came with me.

One thing I found from the BIH seminar was the fear inside me, although I didn't know what it was. After the seminar, I studied the Bible with my small group leader from the seminar.

After a few days, this fear grew inside me. Sometimes, I even had difficulty breathing because of this fear. During those days, I recalled many experiences that I had with my mother.

I was locked inside a room. My mother screamed at me and didn't even let me move. After recalling this, my small group leader told me to forgive my mother. I didn't hate my mother, so I wasn't sure what to forgive. One night, I woke up with this enormous fear, and I suddenly realized what I should forgive about my mother. She shouldn't make me feel scared, even though I was throwing a fit when I was young. No mother should treat their children in that way. I forgave her, and suddenly, the fear was gone.

A few months later, I had another dream. In it, I was screaming at my mother, and she was crying. It reminded me of the grudges that I had against my mother. So I asked God to forgive me.

A few years later, I got married. However, this issue suddenly came out again. My husband is a beautiful man. It was God's blessing that I met him, but I was always anxious about him leaving me. I keep telling him, "Honey. Please don't leave me."

He assured me several times every day that he won't leave me.

My husband worried about my anxiety that he asked

me to meet a shrink. I had sessions with a doctor, but the anxiety wouldn't go away.

Another issue I had was my relationship with my in-laws. I had severe fear and resentment against them. I reminded myself that they loved me and that there's no reason to hate them. However, whenever I heard the word "in-laws," it made me sick. I fell into despair whenever I thought about living close with them and taking care of them when they got older. It felt like I was destined to have a miserable life.

My husband constantly assured me that he would never leave me, but I always had this conviction that he would. So I didn't want to have a baby and tried to find a way to be financially independent. In fact, I spent most of our honeymoon studying to have a job. People thought we were a perfect couple. However, my marriage was full of conflict and stress. Only my parents knew how I was, and they were deeply concerned.

So I came to the BIH seminar again. I wanted to be free from this bondage that held me. It gave me so much pain. I watched people saying,

"God showed me and told me..."

I wished God spoke to me in the same way.

Later, God showed me a scene of my mother that I had never imagined. It was a scene of my mother sitting on the kitchen floor, crying. She just fought with my father. She was in tears, sitting on the corner of the kitchen floor, eating dinner that got cold. She was just swallowing food, and then, suddenly, the word "forgiveness" popped into my head.

"Forgive who? Who should I forgive?"

Right then, I found the hidden anger inside me. It was about my father. I always thought my father was a victim, because he never spoke back to my mother when she shouted at him. So I thought I loved my father, as he was the innocent one, but I realized that there was anger inside me toward my father.

The scene that God showed me happened the day my father and mother fought over issues about his family. When I saw her crying and upset, I felt like my father had chosen his family over my mother. It seemed that he loved his family more than my mother. It looked like he abandoned my mother. It made me so upset.

This scene made me believe that my husband would do the same to me. I believed that he would leave me and abandon me for his family. I had a fear that I would have a life like my mother, lonely and desolate. So I always begged my husband to choose me over his family, but I never sincerely believed he could. I always thought, "He will choose his parents over me."

That's why I hated in-laws so much as I believed they would take my husband from me.

"Now I understand it all..."

I told the counselor what God showed me, and she told me,

"Your life will not be the same as your mother's. Let's

break this idea inside you in the name of Jesus Christ."

I sincerely asked God,

"God. Please don't let my life be like my mother's. Please let me have the beautiful family you intended. I pray in the name of Jesus to break all the anger and grudges of my mother against my father."

I thought I knew everything about myself. But I didn't know about this anger toward my father. God showed me a scene of my mother crying and told me about the anger and fear inside me. It was an amazing experience. I fully understood why my mother was always mad and upset. I realized that there had been no one on her side. I feel so sorry for her. From now on, I'm going to be on her side and be with her. I'm going to wipe off the tears on her face. I will never leave her alone in tears, eating leftovers by herself.

The story of Hyekyung's brother

People have called me a good student, a good son. However, I was not. One day, I saw my father sleeping in my mother's arm. It was the image I had of my father. A weak man who can't protect me. My parents thought I was prudent, but they were wrong. I just didn't like to share things inside me with them. I went to church every Sunday, but felt distant from God by the time I went to college. There was no Jesus in my daily life. I got tired of getting good grades and endless competitions. I lacked energy, but I had no one to share my life with. I felt detached from my parents and everyone else.

One day, my mother went to the BIH seminar, and I noticed changes in her. At first, I thought it was temporary. However, as I saw changes in her life, I became curious about the BIH seminar. I also wanted to know about myself.

When I came to the BIH seminar, God clearly told me what was happening inside me. He showed me two scenes.

One was about what happened when I was young. I was in a bathroom holding five sheets of paper towel. My mother found me and got upset. She told me to use only two sheets. At that time, I thought I was less valuable than five sheets of paper towel.

The other scene was about something that happened when I was at school. One of my classmates had the second-highest score in the class. However, he was afraid of his mother because she wanted him to be at the top of his class. My mother saw him worrying and got mad at me.

"Look! Learn from that kid! That's the attitude you should have to get a high score. I don't know what to do with you anymore."

So later, when I got a low test score, I faked crying, and my mother got upset.

"Look at you! What kind of man on earth cries because of a test score?"

These were the two scenes God showed me. At first, I

didn't get why he showed them to me. But soon, I understood their severe impact on my inner being.

One was telling me about how I valued myself. That incident made me think that I didn't deserve to have five pieces of paper towels. I felt so insecure about myself. So to be better than who I was, I studied so hard. But when I came to college, my classmates were far better than I was, and it made me feel like a failure.

The other one was telling me about my mother's attitude that I hated. She was inconsistent, and it confused me. I felt like I couldn't make her happy. It resulted in despair inside me, and I felt the same way with God. I became very skeptical about God when I came to college because of his inconsistency. He gave Abraham a son but told him to sacrifice his son. He was just like my mother, who always asked whatever she wanted and never considered others' feelings.

I didn't feel safe and secure about believing in God, who was temperamental. So I found two things that I could trust: good grades and a degree. Indeed, they were the only things I could trust in my life. I was always in a severely competitive mode and anxious about getting a good grade and degree. What I learned from the BIH seminar gave me a new perspective on God and myself. Now, I trust God in my life. I have been set free from the pressures that previously devastated my life.

SEXUAL ISSUES THAT CAUSE SEVERE DAMAGE AND THE ROLE OF INNER HEALING

Most of the severe issues that people shared during the BIH seminar were related to sexual issues. While we decided not to publicly share those cases related to sexual assault, it has been the top cause of deep wounds in many of the seminar's participants.

Unfortunately, many people from the BIH seminar were exposed to sexual violence, and most of the assaults occurred during their childhood. It was devastating to know that a significant portion of the identified offenders consisted of relatives or people they were close to. Sexual assault brings fatal damages and wounds to one's life in their worst forms. It has a lasting impact on one's personality and character.

The only way to heal the wound from sexual assaults is through the power of the Holy Spirit and the Cross of Jesus Christ.

We have witnessed several participants who have been relieved of these fatal wounds.

CASE

The story of "A"

She was a nurse taking time off due to her health issues. She went to a mental institution, took pills, and had therapies. However, she didn't get better.

She attempted to kill herself with hydrochloric acid. It damaged her throat, and she was sent to a mental institution. It is a miracle that she is still alive.

When we started the session with her, she was newly married, but she didn't have any joy or hope in her life. So she attempted suicide again soon after her wedding. When we met her, her eyes were empty. She was gazing into space with a fixed smile on her face. I prayed to God to tell me what made her like this.

Soon we started talking. I found out that she felt herself very dirty. She told me that she was raped by her relative when she was young. The offender died many years ago, but the pain was still vivid inside her.

"I was too young to know what was happening, but I

could know that I was dirty and that something was wrong. I felt like I shouldn't say anything about this to anyone. So I didn't. The funny thing was because I felt dirty, I became sexually promiscuous. I thought I wanted to make myself dirtier."

She was overwhelmed with guilt for her promiscuous behavior. As she felt more guilty, the pain grew in her. With continued pain inside her, she became insensitive to pain. Nothing meant anything to her. There's no reason for her to live. She tried to kill herself, but it didn't work. Nothing changed.

"But I haven't felt any impact from that incident. I don't even have any grudges toward the person who assaulted me. He just made a mistake. He didn't know what he was doing."

She was wrong. The incident happened to her. It had impacted her life, but she didn't want to speak about it before God or show her emotions.

There is a will to live inside people. At the same time, a suicide attempt can be a painful way of showing one's will to cleanse and renew oneself.

I explained how and why God wanted to renew her mind. I prayed to God to do something new regarding the assault. She hesitated at first but then decided to pray with me. While we were praying, I saw deep sorrow hidden inside her come out. She spoke to God about things that she had buried. It was so painful for her to speak out. I noticed that God touched her heart when she told God everything inside her. She started to cry. She hadn't cried for years. This time, it was tears of joy.

"I felt something different. When I was talking to God, I saw that he changed what happened that night. It was a dark night, but God was there, and suddenly, the morning came."

We don't know what exactly she meant by that, but I knew the Holy Spirit did something powerful inside her. Only God can touch her despair and renew her mind. I felt like her blank eyes started to shine.

A few days later, she called me, saying,

"Now, I can go to church. It is still difficult to pray, but I feel calm and good. Before, I couldn't attend church because I felt so dirty about myself."

She came to the BIH seminar after that. She told me that although she forgave the offender who hurt her, she still found it difficult to see herself as a victim. She thought it was her fault, or something was wrong with her that she was assaulted. She was still blaming herself for everything and hurting herself. She had this belief deep inside her, saying that God also hated her because she was dirty. This is the typical deception of a demon toward victims of sexual assaults.

It would take time for her to know and see herself in the eyes of God. However, what matters is that she has started to open her heart to God and harbors hope that she could be renewed through him.

CASE

The story of "B"

B found it challenging to stay at the BIH seminar. She was beautiful, but there was an angry look on her face. I had a private session with her.

"It is not my first time coming to the BIH seminar, but I still find it difficult to see what's wrong with me. I feel so disappointed that the seminar will be over soon and that I will come home with nothing. Now, I am skeptical about the seminar. It's like creating some issues that don't even exist."

She became upset as she spoke to me, but I felt like she was actually asking for help. She came to the seminar and wanted to have a private session. What does she need? So I asked her,

"Can you tell me anything?"

She seemed confused but said,

"Well... It was tough for me to come here and talk to you, but I couldn't let myself go back home without anything. I felt desperate. I am not sure what I need to tell you. So I'll just try."

I asked God for help in my mind and then proceeded to ask her.

"What did you pray for during the seminar?"

"Issues in me. Issues about my personality. It has been so difficult for me to have an open heart. I think it is my issue that needed to be fixed. But I don't know how. It's just getting complicated."

"And what else?"

"A student in my class."

"What is your concern about her?"

"It's…she is…"

She started to talk about many things concerning a female student in the class that she was teaching. However, I felt like she was not sharing what actually mattered. I was still wondering what it was. I prayed in my mind, and she started to share the painful experience she had.

Her close relative raped her, and she was concerned that the student in her class might have had the exact same experience.

She had a life full of criticism and blamed others. She couldn't handle herself watching older people, seniors, or bosses in her work make mistakes. As a result, people left her, and she became more furious with others.

"Have you ever prayed for the assault?"

"No! For what? I just wanted to remove it from my memory. It's just water under the bridge. Prayers can't change the past."

"You're wrong. You can bring the issue before God. He is a creator. He will do things that no one else can."

"What would he do?"

"We don't know. But one thing for sure is that he will do something inside you. If there's anything that God can't handle or solve, then he is not an almighty God. Do you think God is almighty?"

"Yes, I do."

"Then why don't you tell God about it? Let him do the next step."

We started to pray together about the darkest thing inside her mind. While crying, she shared how she felt powerless and how scared she was. While we were praying, I saw changes in her look. I started to notice that God was doing something in her.

"God gave me a new dress, and he is holding my hand and taking me to a new place bathed in bright sunlight."

She told me in tears.

CASE

The story of "C"

C shared with her best friend an experience she had, but this friend just told her to let it go.

"Just forget about it. You were young, and you didn't know what it was. There's no good to keep thinking about it."

So C decided to let it go, and she did. However, the issue came up again while she was married. She had trouble having sex with her husband. It felt like torture. She avoided her husband and soon faced problems in her marriage.

As a result, her husband felt abandoned and got hurt, but he found it difficult to express his feelings. He volunteered to be transferred to a branch office and moved out. Thus, only a few months after their wedding, the couple were separated. He started to date another woman, and C stayed home alone, only focused on church work. She thought that all issues in her marriage were her husband's fault. She met someone at church, and they became close, but as a Christian, she felt severe guilt about having a divorce.

She was confused. When she came to the BIH seminar, she got so mad for no reason. She wanted to confess and repent, but she felt so much anger that she couldn't pray. She repented for having a relationship outside of marriage, but it didn't make her feel better.

She felt like God was rejecting her prayer. So she asked for a private session and shared her story.

"I want to pray. But I can't. I feel like God rejects my prayer for forgiveness."

"Do you have anything that you want to be forgiven?"

"Yes. I loved a man, and he is not my husband."

"Is it what you want to be forgiven for?"

"Well…why do you ask?"

"I feel like there's something else."

"When I came to the seminar, I recall some memory I had when I was young. It made me feel confused. I didn't know how to handle it. It was something I didn't want to discuss or think about. I came here to save my marriage, and this memory kept distracting me from praying. It was so annoying that I almost decided to go home."

"I think God allowed you remember the incident because it is important to reconcile your relationship with your husband. Can you tell me what it is?"

She found it very hard to share at first, but later on, she told me that it happened when she was young. She and her friends performed some sexual acts, and she felt guilty and ashamed that she enjoyed doing them. She was afraid of praying about it.

"I...I asked my friends to do that. I thought it was just for fun. I feel so ashamed of myself."

The shame and guilt in her blocked her from praying to God. She needed to forgive herself.

"God told us that he will forgive our sin if we confess. Do you confess that you made sin?"

"Yes, I do."

She asked for forgiveness from God and forgave herself. Later, she told me that she and her husband had a successful martial reconciliation.

Wounds from sexual issues and their impacts

A victim of a sexual violation often has two contrasting feelings: feeling dirty and harming themselves in a sexual way.

The Bible says that sexual assaults result in a victim being exposed to sexual sin. Often, it results in a victim being obsessed with sex in a sinful way. It can even lead to continued obscene thoughts and masturbation. When it happens, victims start to have guilt and feel ashamed of themselves. With guilt and shame, a victim becomes vulnerable to temptation and is motivated to commit sexual sins. There's death at the end of such guilt.

At the same time, some victims become obsessed with cleaning themselves after the assault. They can't stand their messy house, dust on their clothes, and so on. It also leads them to experience severe stress in their relationships with others.

Sexual assaults leave traumatic pain to victims, such that they have to seek outside help and counseling to achieve healing. Unfortunately, many victims of sexual violations avoid seeking help or counseling due to shame. Many victims are also skeptical about the help and role of God, as the assault has already happened.

However, God can handle and solve any issues inside us. His power is beyond our expectations. The demon continues to destroy and harm us through sex, because it is the most precious part of a human that creates life. Therefore, its impact on humans is also crucial. Sexual issues and wounds can't be hidden for long. They impact other parts of one's life and attack their vulnerable parts. It is a blind spot where the demon comes and attacks our minds.

The Holy Spirit is the only answer to take care of this blind spot inside us. The Spirit cleanses and heals the sinful spot inside us and turns it into a holy place. As we have learned in an earlier section, Jesus experienced all the violence and pains that damaged his dignity, and for this reason, he can connect with victims of sexual violence. He flows and spreads his healing power to us, and he wants you to be with him and stand next to him.

The Holy Spirit who makes the power of healing flow is with you right now.